W. HOCK HOCHHEIM'S

HAND, STICK, KNIFE, GUN
CLOSE QUARTER COMBATIVES

TRAINING MISSION ONE

CQCG

Lauric Press

CLOSE QUARTER COMBAT GROUP
TRAINING MISSION ONE

by W. Hock Hochheim

Also by W. Hock Hochheim

The Foundation: Knife Fighting Encyclopedia Volume 1
Military Knife Combat: Knife Fighting Encyclopedia Volume 2
Unarmed Versus the Knife: Knife Fighting Encyclopedia Volume 3
Shooting from the Hip
Punches (fiction)
Find Missing Persons
The Great Escapes of Pancho Villa
Knife Counter/Knife Combatives
Training Mission Two
Training Mission Three
Training Mission Four
Training Mission Five
Be Bad Now (fiction)
My Gun is My Passport (fiction)
Copyright September, 2002, 2011
All rights reserved.

ISBN Number: 978-1932113-48-8
Recorded in the United States Library of Congress

WARNING!

The author, publisher or seller will not and does not assume any responsibility for the use or misuse of information contained in this book. The one and only purpose of this publication is to provide information for the purpose of self-defense against illegal aggression. Use your knife only to save your life and/or the lives of others. Use the information only when it is morally, legally and ethically appropriate to do so.

Table of Contents

The Close Quarter Combat Group
from Epiphany to Doctrine

Epiphany

I saw it all coming together into the true essence of combat. I came to understand the only reason I learned and taught fighting systems was to defeat two targets, the enemy soldier and the criminal, not to pass on grandmaster dynasties or to preserve art for the sake of tradition. There are two ways to defeat the enemy: less-than-lethal means and lethal means. In short, sometimes we take them prisoner and sometimes we have to kill them. A competent warrior, whether a citizen, police officer or soldier, may do each as legally, morally and ethically needed.

No one system, or discipline, such as the military sciences, holds all the answers. I began to forge a course that bridges the gap between the police, the military, the martial artists and the aware citizenry. To structure it as realistically as possible, I used a *reverse-engineering* approach by starting with the fight first and working backward in probabilities.

In the Year 2000 I began to organize all my fighting tactics and strategies into one comprehensive, blended program called the Close Quarter Combatives Group. The CQCG is made up of four primary foundations, my four separate 10 level courses:

- Unarmed Combatives Course
- Knife/Counter-Knife Course
- SDMS Impact Weapon Course
- Gun/Counter-Gun Course

CQC Group Rank and Instructorships

Various rankings in each or all the courses can be achieved in seminars and classes. Train with us and master these levels. CQCG Instructorships involve classroom training, hands-on practice and both written and physical testing in a designated camp or course.

Basic CQCG Instructor   *upon completing Level 3*
Advanced CQCG Instructor   *upon completing Level 6*
Expert CQCG Instructor   *upon completing Level 9*
Master CQCG Instructor   *upon completing Level 10*

Re-certification

As always, you must maintain proper ethical and moral standards. You must not be a criminal nor be attached to any radical or questionable organization of this or any nation. I need to know that you continue to work out, teach, learn and grow. I need to see you in a training session once every 12 months minimum. These are the standards I demand.

My Training Promise to You

Civilian and martial arts courses are almost always off-base with real world needs and unplugged into the newest, scientific trends of combating enemy soldiers, terrorists and criminals. Martial arts dynasties must be perpetuated. Traditions must be upheld. Military and police academies must spend their time with political and non-combat related training agendas. SEALS need to swim. Rangers and Reconn need to reconnoiter. Berets must master commo *[communications]*. Police need to understand traffic accident reporting. The list of non-combat training subject requirements for these groups is almost endless. There are classes on saluting, organized hazing and harassment, marching, etc. that subtract precious time from specific combatives study. Even courses designated as combat courses waste time on jumping jacks, marching and other steps to develop physical fitness. A true warrior is fit, comes fit and remains fit on his own time. As a result, 100 hours of training may contain only 40 hours of actual combat tactics.

The CQC Group training mission books, with this the first of 10 books, set forth comprehensive and insightful training doctrine and methodologies unlike any other. We bridge the gap between the military, the police, the martial artist and the aware citizenry. I have interfaced with many members of these organizations around the world. I am convinced this CQC course is the most comprehensive, complete, scientific, hand stick knife and gun, close quarter course in the world, bar none. Anywhere. This is my promise. Best of the best, forged from the best disciplines.

Epiphany.
It is all here for you already.
Are you ready for the next step?

CQCG

Doctrine

Unarmed Combatives Strike 1:
The Finger Strike Attack Module

Finger Strike Overview

The martial arts raise the visage of ancient, bald supermen ramming straight fingers into buckets of sand and pebbles to break tiles and boards with thrusting finger attacks. But in reality using your fingers as an impact tool for a target other than the eyes or extremely soft, specific body spots asks for trouble in the form of sprains and breaks. Average, normal fingers cannot ram into the bones of the body or break cinder blocks. Instead, they may rake and thrust into the eyes, slap noses and twist skin with speed and accuracy. The finger-to-eye strike is the essential bread and butter survival tool. It provides the mainstay of rape prevention and a primer vs. the terrorists, criminals and enemy soldiers.

Finger Strike Studies and Observations 1) Empathy and Combat

"I'll poke him right in the eye!" declares both the braggart and/or the housewife, raising the visage of this famous self-defense technique. The braggart perches on his stool at the local tavern, talking tough. The woman imagines fighting a rapist. And true, the eye attack is a devastating tool. Even King Kong raging atop the Empire State Building would suffer if his eyes were hit by the machine guns mounted on the famous bi-planes attacking him. In fact, finger-to-eye attacks have been successful against sharks and alligators.

We've all seen the movies. The protagonists do battle with their hands smeared all over each other's faces, pushing against the heads. Jaws grimace. The necks strain to explosion in resistance. You scream from your couch or from the theater seat with frustration.

"Poke him in the eye, for God's sakes!" knowing what quick results will befall this Hannibal Lector if blinded. But then the two-hour movie would become a mere 60 minutes with a timely eye attack!

Executing this or any other severe tactic under the stress of combat and against a real person however, has psychological implications above and beyond the simple physical act. The study of human violence has many layers, and one is empathy.

The dictionary defines empathy as "the action of understanding, being aware of, being sensitive to and vicariously experiencing the feelings, thoughts and experience of another." Normal, psychologically healthy people have empathy. Often we wince at the prospect of people hurt in sports, crime, accidents and war. The limb break in football, the body squashed in a car wreck, the pulverized victims of the plane crash – these events hypnotize us and make us gasp. Whether we realize it or not, we have a "feeling" for the person during the seconds of pain, shock and death. We imagine the surviving families and friends. Few truly walk away from a funeral without the passing relief buried deep in our psyches – "at least it wasn't me," or "at least I didn't get that cancer," …and so on. Empathy and these compassionate roots of empathy connect us as human beings.

Years ago, before the world became so politically correct, before the science of killing people for survival became buried in make-happy-face, pop jargon, some very hard core military units experimented with various gruesome training methods. Trainers would acquire bushels of grapefruits and pass them out to their troops. The drill? The soldier holds the grapefruit in the palms of his two hands, and with both thumbs proceeds to gouge two deep holes into the pulp. This was to simulate an eye gauge and offer the student the real wet feeling of the process. Warm grapefruits were better. Some units went so far as to tape the grapefruits to the faces of half their men, and the remaining soldiers would now attack a life-sized target, ramming their thumbs in the same areas as the real eyes. Documents report that even some of the toughest characters, many veterans of prior wars, winced at this process. Yet, the simple, physical movement is not unlike peeling that grapefruit or orange while sitting on your back porch.

Faced with this CQC encounter, would the men actually do this? Few have. Why do many shutter at the idea of gouging an eye out, cutting a throat or shooting a face? One main reason is this empathy. We imagine the experience, if even for a split second on a primal level, what it would be like to have our own eyes gouged. To lose a kneecap. A hand. To see our blood spray from our neck. We hesitate. And in doing so, this empathy can get you killed!

Should trainers ask a person to shed their empathy? NO! In order to become a whole and complete person, one who builds and supports a world of freedom, safety and justice, you need empathy and compassion as essential characteristics. Without it, YOU would become the next Hannibal Lector, Stalin, or Herman Goering. All I ask is that you see and understand this big picture and park empathy aside when action is needed. Psychologists often call this *compartmentalizing*. To live and survive in true lethal combat, we must train our mind and body to overcome these empathetic inhibitions for those horrible, dark moments of worst-case scenarios. We have to see the devil for what he is, call the devil a devil, look the devil right in the eyes…and then rip his eyes out.

*The finger-to-eye is the **Mission One** hand strike, the great diminisher and disabler.*

Finger Strike Studies and Observations 2) Finger Strikes – Basic Execution
There are three basic kinds of finger positions and three kinds of finger strike attacks. There are raking positions, spear positions and thumb gouge positions and hooking, thrusting and ripping attacks. All will be displayed with training methods.

The Finger Positions

FP 1) Fingers spread in a rake formation

FP 2) Fingers together in a spear formation

FP 3) Thumb or other finger spread from hand

– for gouging
– for ripping

The Finger Attacks

FA 1) Hooking motions, as in eye jabs and slaps

FA 2) Thrusting

FA 3) Pinching and/or ripping and twisting with the fingers

Finger Formation 1) Rake. Fingers spread apart and partially bent. This prevents the fingers from being jammed and increases the range like a shotgun pattern. If the enemy ducks or shifts away, the spread fingers may allow for one of the fingers to still catch in and around the eye.

Finger Formation 2) Spear. Fingers are formed to brace together like the head of a spear. The side supports of finger against finger may prevent sprains. Always partially bend your fingers to give them some spring. Tuck the thumb to prevent snagging it on the enemy's blocks.

Finger Formation 3) Thumb Gouge. Position the thumb beside the rest of the hand to attack the eyes. This is done with one or two hands.

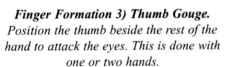

Finger Attack 1) The Hooking Strike

Hooking finger slaps to the bridge of the nose may cause great diminishment in the enemy. Eyes water. The nose resonates with stunning pain. A finger slap to the face may be effective. Hooking fingers that rake in and around the eyes may be very effective. The range of results from hitting around the eyes causing distraction to some worst-case histories where pupils are cut open by fingernails. The hooking fingers may also rip the eyeglasses off the face, impairing vision or setting up a direct unobstructed attack to the eyes. They can rip goggles off their proper position. Dislodged goggles, depending upon their end position on the enemy's face may distract and impair vision, and give you a temporary, slight advantage. A harsh, hooking slap across the bridge of a nose may provide a devastating, stunning strike.

Finger Attack 2) The Thrust

Thrusting spear hands or thrusting thumbs drive straight to the eyes or throat. Thrusting fingers into other body targets may sprain your fingers.

Finger Attack 3) Pinching: Twists, Fish Hook Rips and Pulls to the Mouth

One additional use of the finger attack is any grab and/or pull. This ripping finger attack may be used to control a person or cause serious injury. Just watch the teeth. This finger catch is usually done after the fighters are in extreme close quarters, standing or on the ground. The fingers may also grip and twist the flesh. Beware, because this may only further enrage an assailant.

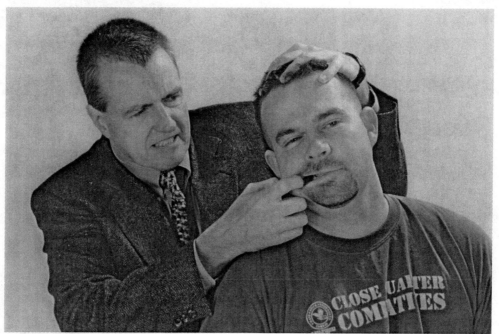

A one finger Fish Hook. Obviously watch out for a bite, but a catch, pinch and rip of the check with one or more fingers can be devastating, creating an avulsion—when a piece of tissue or skin is torn loose or pulled off. A hooking finger can also simply maneuver and control the enemy.

Finger Attack Synergy Drills

Synergy drills develop execution skill. They develop total body performance by doing the tactic in the air, then hitting hard objects to develop power and feel resistance. Use focus mitts or other training apparatuses.

     Synergy Drill 1: Solo command and mastery in the air
     Synergy Drill 2: Solo command and mastery striking objects for speed and power
     Synergy Drill 3: Flow and skill drills with partners

Your final product is standing, kneeling and ground combat scenarios. The following are the finger attack solo command and mastery drills.

Drill 1) Solo Command and Mastery of the Finger Attacks

Obtain the fundamentals, full command and physical mastery of the finger strike. Practice the raking hook attack and the thrusting attack using points on a clock as reference. Start high, low or either side as though you were looking at a clock and fire finger attacks.

C&M Series 1) The Hooking Finger Strike

Raking/hook attack fingers from the 12 o'clock or high position.

Raking, hook attack fingers from the 3 o'clock or right side position.

Raking, hook attack fingers from the 6 o'clock or low position.

Raking, hook attack fingers from the 9 o'clock or left side.

C & M Series 2) The Thrusting Finger Strike

These strikes come on as straight a line as possible, from original hand position to target. Use a trick to set up the attack. Scratch your head for the 12 o'clock set up. Reach into a breast pocket. Hook a thumb atop your belt buckle. These appear to be non-aggressive, typical movements that position your hands closer for a sudden attack.

Thrusting finger strike from a 12 o'clock or high position.

Thrusting finger strike from a 3 o'clock or right side position.

Thrusting finger strike from a 6 o'clock or low position.

Thrusting finger strike from a 9 o'clock or left side position.

C & M Series 3) The Thumb Gouge Series

There are single-hand and double-hand eye gouges.

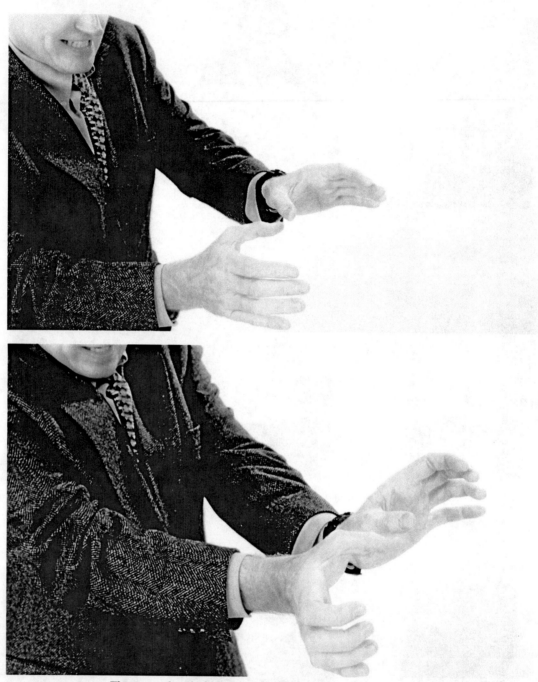

Thrust two hands forward and then rotate thumbs in for insertion.

There are single hand and double hand eye gouge strikes. This type of strike potentially allows for considerable stunning impact to the head from the rest of the hand. (Palm strikes are the subject strike of *CQCG Training Mission Two.)*

Finger Attack Variation Training

You must practice all these with both the left and right hands. Work these formations standing, kneeling and on the ground. Work these finger strikes against a partner flashing a focus mitt. Work these finger strikes against heavy bags or similar items to feel realistic resistance and develop goal-specific strength. Working against a face model with eyes would be best.

Drill 2) Partner Finger Attack Power and Speed Drills

Set 1) Focus Mitt Drills

Focus mitts are primarily for speed development. This series of mitt drills develop these speed skills for the eye jab. However, due to the limited nature and force of the finger-to-eye attack, the drill may be done with a trainer simply flashing an open palm instead of a focus mitt.

Focus Mitt Drill Set 1) Mitt Strikes

The trainer holds a mitt up. You practice striking the mitt.

Focus Mitt Drill Set 2) Flashing Mitt Strikes

The trainer flashes the mitt quickly open and shut down upon his chest. The faster he flashes the mitt, the harder it is to strike, and the faster the practitioner will become. Start slowly and increase flashing speed.

Focus Mitt Drill Set 3) Sparring Mitt Strikes

The trainer moves in a sparring manner and flashes the mitt. The trainer may decide to give you some flak by striking and kicking back at you.

Set 2) Statue Drills

The statue drill provides a new practitioner an excellent introduction to the basics movements of hand attacks in relation with the limbs of an opponent. The trainer stands before you with his arms up and out like a statue. The statue stands before the student as in the photo to the right. This is an arms-high example. In some cases, one needs the arms to be positioned lower.

The trainer stands much like the classic Chinese training dummy, and you train these techniques in their simplest form.

You work the arm-to-arm contact and finger strike across the arms in the following inside and outside practice progression, creating complete lines of familiarity. You may practice your arm-to-arm contact two ways: a back-handed style contact or a cross-your-body style contact. These may be done aggressively or defensively.

Contact 1) You are outside the right arm
Contact 2) Your are inside the right arm
Contact 3) You are inside the left arm
Contact 4) You are outside the left arm

The Back-Hand or Back-Arm Contact and Eye Attack

Make contact from the tops of the fingers down to the elbow in this category. Do not close your hand into a fist, but put strength into the fingers. Whether you are inside or outside the opponent's arms, this movement is a possibility. This movement may include any of the strikes and will be used throughout the CQC Group course.

Solo Practice: A high back-handed entry with eye jab. First a high contact. Next, a low contact.

The Palm/Cross-Arm Contact and Eye Attack

The arm makes contact starting from the fingers, palm, on to the forearm in a movement that crosses your body. Whether you are inside or outside the opponent's arms, this movement is a possibility. This movement may include any of the unarmed combatives strikes and will be used throughout the CQC Group course.

A Palm/Cross-Arm contact entry and eye jab set-up. A sample study.

For the complete Finger Strike Statue Drill Progression you must practice by working across the arm formation:

     1) With a Back-Hand/Back-Arm contact. Strike on the high line.
     2) With a Back-Hand/Back-Arm contact. Strike on the low line.
     3) With a Palm/Cross-Arm contact. Strike on the high line:
              – over the arm eye attack
              – under the arm eye attack

     4) With a Palm/Cross-Arm contact. Strike on the low line.

The following photo series examples will display some of these statue sets, enough for you to understand the process. The trainer must keep his arms in position to avoid a natural tendency to drift too far apart from each other. The forearm will strike the limb with force enough to clear a path for the eye attack. We use the word *contact* because the arm-to-arm connection may represent either an aggressive, preemptive strike on your part, or a defensive block against an attack.

     We will study palm-strike/inner arm contact in ***CQCG Training Mission Two.***

Finger Strike Statue Drill – A Sample: Over the Arm Eye Attack Series
Here you will use a Palm/Cross-Arm contact and the finger strike will assault over the connecting arms.

Cross contact and strike over the top, from outside the trainer's right arm.

Cross contact and strike over the top, from inside the trainer's right arm.

Cross contact and strike over the top, from inside the trainer's left arm.

Cross contact and strike over the top, from outside the trainer's left arm.

Finger Strike Statue Drill – A Sample: Under the Arm Eye Attack Series
Here you will use a Palm/Cross-Arm Contact and the finger strike will assault over the connection. Ram the opponent's arm with your attack forearm to ensure success.

Cross contact and strike under the arms (in this case just under your arm) from outside the trainer's right arm.

Cross contact and strike under the arms, from inside the trainer's right arm.

Cross contact and strike under the arms, from inside the trainer's left arm.

Cross contact and strike under the arms, from outside the trainer's left arm.

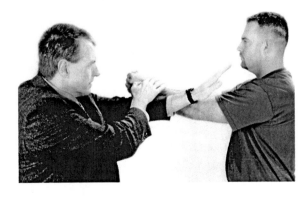

Finger Strike Statue Drill – A Sample: The Low Line Series

The statue drill can simulate low body punches. You modify your contact with a low response. In this sample we use the Backhand/Back Arm response. Your eye attack will zero in above the connecting arms. With low line attacks there can be no *under the arm* eye attacks because the arm-to-arm contact point is too low.

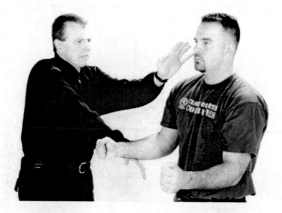

Back arm contact and strike over the top, from outside the trainer's right arm.

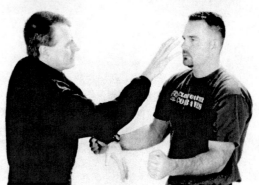

Back arm contact and strike over the top, from inside the trainer's right arm.

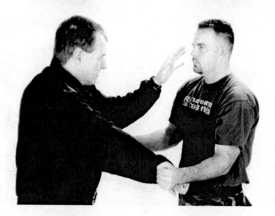

Back arm contact and strike over the top, from inside the trainer's left arm.

Back arm contact and strike over the top, from outside the trainer's left arm.

Set 3) Statue Pumping Drill

In the next skill developing drill, the trainer now pumps the arms, slowly at first, and the trainee learns to work the tactic in real time. As the practitioner improves, have your *statue* take more realistic poses that will eventually lead to combat scenarios.

Set 4) The Block, Pass and Pin Drill

This drill is exercised in various martial arts systems. This type of skill drill may prove invaluable in building coordination, speed, strength and target acquisition. The Block, Pass and Pin Drill takes six steps, or beats, between two partners. Partners first master the six steps/beats. Then one executes half-beat inserts where possible. Here are the six steps done solo in the air.

Step/Beat 1: You block an incoming left side attack with a left block.

Step/Beat 2: Your right hand sweeps clockwise and sweeps down the strike.

Step/Beat 3: Your right hand slaps down the passed strike.

Step/Beat 4: To continue the flow of the drill, you strike your training partner. He blocks.

Step/Beat 5: He passes you down with his own clockwise movement.

Step/Beat 6: He pins you down. Next he will strike you, and you will block with step 1.

Here is the Block, Pass and Pin Drill done with a partner. Since we are studying the eye jab at this level, the opponent will also strike at you with a high raking/hooking eye jab.

Step/Beat 1: *His right hand attacks with a raking/ hooking attack. You stop it with your left arm.*

Step/Beat 2: *Your right hand circles in and passes the attack.*

Step/Beat 3: *Your left hand pins the attack.*

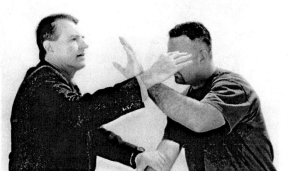

Step/Beat 4: *You now attack him in the same manner, reversing the pattern. He blocks.*

Step/Beat 5: *He passes.*

Step/Beat 6: *He pins, and he repeats process.*

Variations: Half Beat Insert Attacks to the Block, Pass and Pin Drill – Samples

With this 6 Step/Beat format or tempo established, now begin the eye jab inserts on the half-beats of the six steps.

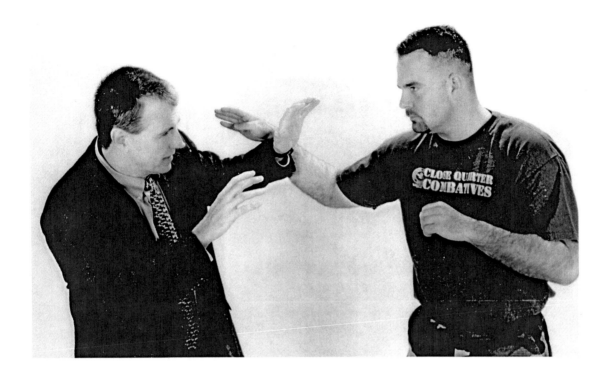

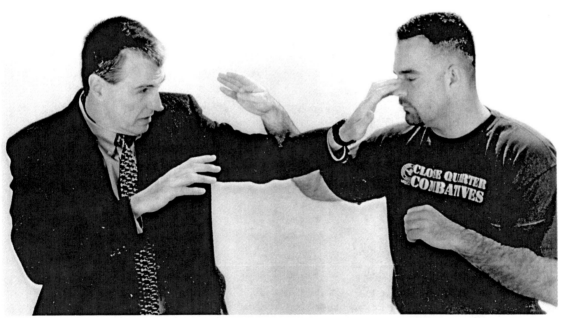

On beat 1 1/2 insert an eye strike. You have made your blocking contact to stop his incoming eye jab for Step/Beat 1. You slide your forearm across his forearm in a sawing fashion straight into an eye jab.

*Here is how it might be done vs. a knife attack. Next, you would use
follow-up tactics as prescribed in this CQC Group course.*

*Here is a half beat counter attack eye jab with the OTHER hand, as expressed
vs. an impact weapon attack. You would then follow-up with the many grappling techniques
demonstrated in the rest of the CQCG course.*

On Step/Beat 2 1/2, insert an eye strike. You have blocked and are passing the attack.
Your right hand passes and then shoots forward into an eye jab. Try to keep your
forearm in contact with his forearm, almost as though you are sawing up his arm. This
may hold his arm in place, or at least alert you that it is moving.

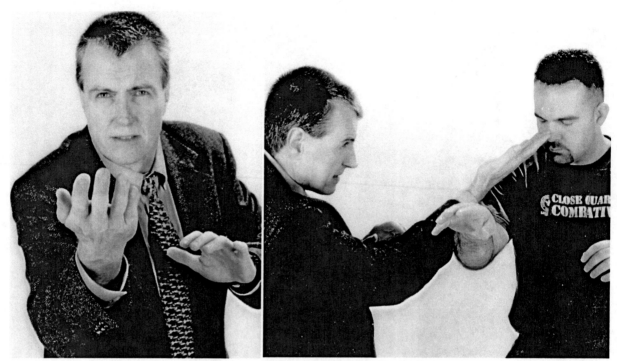

Sometimes a palm up eye strike may be timely.

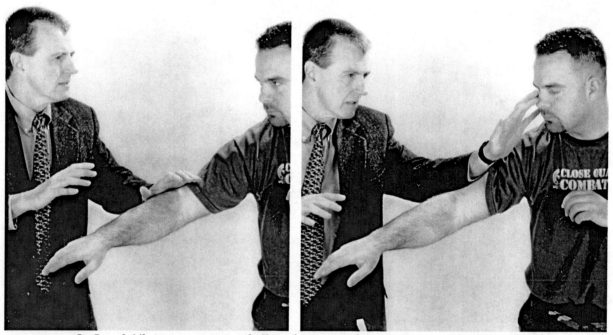

On Beat 3 1/2, insert an eye attack. Keep that sawing forearm in contact if at all possible.

Variation Drills

Variation 1: All Three Drill: Try to quickly do all three inserts in the same six beats. Start with doing one. Then add two. Finally, do three insert eye jabs inside the six beat drill.

Variation 2: Weapons Drill. The trainer holds a knife or stick during the drill.

Variation 3: Remember that this block, pass and pin pattern can and must be practiced from all four corners of the torso.

Variation 4: The drill must also be practiced in ground combat positions, on your back and sides.

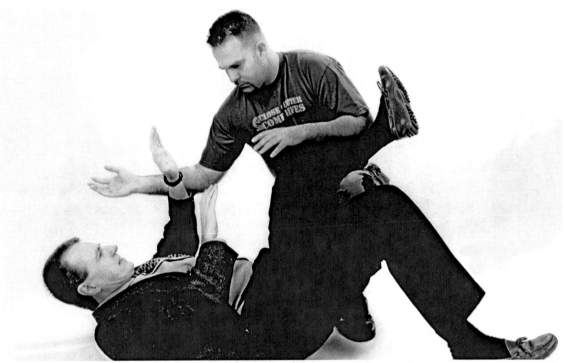

You must develop side-to-side and on-your-back skill. Try all these drills in ground positions.

Set 5) The Clinch Drill

Both parties will start apart, then clash together into the classic grappling clinch position. As soon as possible, the trainee seeks an eye jab.

The confrontation. The charge into the classic fighter's clinch. Here the trainee delivers a thumb gouge.

Set 6) Ground Fight Roll Drill: Eye Attack Development

The two practitioners may start in any ground position they choose. The trainer wears very effective eye protection. Both begin to wrestle. Whenever possible, you will attack the eyes. Practice at increasing speeds and strength as skill develops. Important! See just how often an eye attack comes available in a ground fight.

Three Counters to an Eye Attack

1) Gear. Wearing the proper gear from eyeglasses, sunglasses to protective glasses is important when you go into combat.

2) Block. One block is getting your hand or forearm up to block as a counter. The open and spread finger attack may be hung up with a block.

3) The duck and squint. If given a second, you will reflexively save your eyes with sudden head and eye movements.

Finger Attack Option Awareness
Combat Scenarios

The previous study and practice have given you a working knowledge of the finger strike usage, but in order to complete the module you must make the eye attack function inside combat scenarios. Here are just a few samples. Remember combat scenarios end with the enemy on the ground and out of the fight. These fight finishing movements are demonstrated throughout the CQCG Course.

CS 1) Aggressive Sample Study
In this preemptive movement, you take aggressive action.

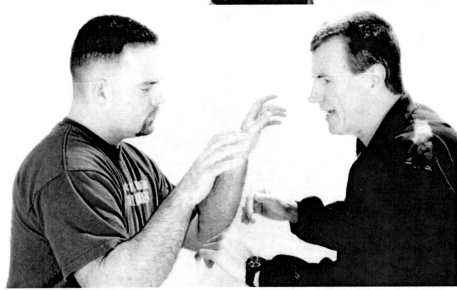

The conflict begins. You deflect the enemy's arms out with forearm attacks to his arms to clear a path to the eyes. You attack the eyes.

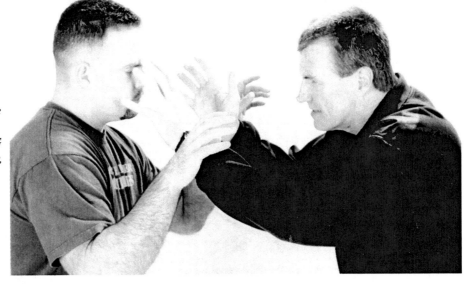

You then execute multiple hits and any finishes shown later in the CQCG course. Finish as morally, ethically or legally needed.

CS 2)
A Defensive -
Sample Study

You take defensive action. The conflict begins. He attacks.

You block an attack and set-up to execute a finger attack with the arm that blocked.

You then execute multiple hits. Finish as morally, ethically or legally needed.

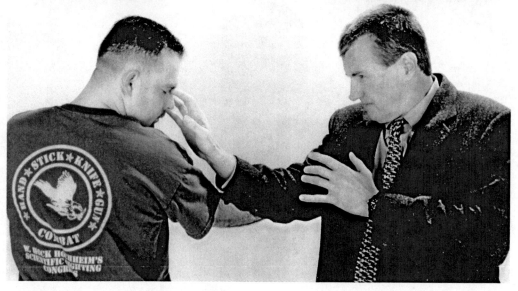

CS 3) Eye Jab Counters the Common Headlock – A Sample Study

This eye attack helps you escape the common headlock grabs. It is a classic scenario taught in all good military and martial fighting systems. The actual street or battlefield headlock is a chaotic, stumbling conflict. The attacker usually pummels your head blindly. Many break parts of their hands doing this.

We will dissect head locks, cranks and neck attacks in painstaking detail in later CQCG training books, but now we will explore two common grappling attacks to the neck: a restraint that just holds you there and a choke that is a squeeze on your neck. Most head locks are just restraints either on purpose or ignorant attempts at choking. Head locks are very common captures, found in the street fight, the hockey match and the baseball game. Watch these scraps and see how chaotic they really are. Untrained fighters will often hurt their hands banging your skull as your face is often well down and partially covered by clothing.

1) The enemy has you in the common guillotine headlock. Often, this is more of a restraint than a choke, but could be either. He begins the common skull punching. Often his far arm pummels your hand and face.

2) You stabilize yourself and focus on an eye attack. Reach around back with your inside arm. Striking the groin is an option with your inside arm, but getting at the eyes is a quick fix.

3) Attack the eyes. Dig until it works. This sudden attack should cause the enemy to let loose with one hand of the headlock or quit the punching. With this eye distraction, try to pry the headlock open.

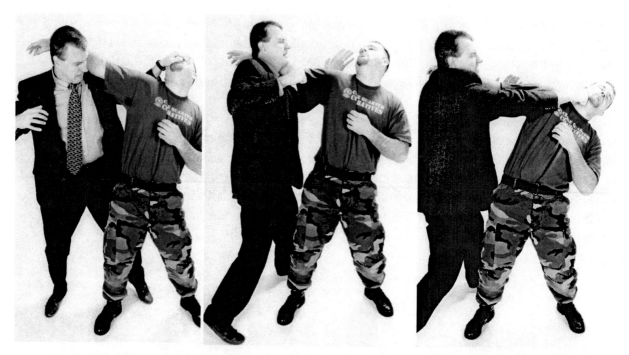

Get a second grip on the eye and face area, stand up with all your torso strength. Turn your body into him for power. Pull him back. Belt him. Finish as morally, ethically or legally needed. Here is a sledgehammer punch to the side of the neck to knock him cold. Barrage as needed.

CS 4: Escape the Ground Choke – A Sample Study

Here you and your training partner (with eye protection) start in a worst-case situation. You are downed, and he already has you in a choke. This is your starting point. Try to keep your windpipe or at least one carotid open. Then this becomes a neck restraint rather than a choke. Getting your chin inside the arm is a good option if the choke has not settled in. Trench your chin in. If his arm is bare, spit down on his forearm to cause a slippery slope for your chin to slip inside his forearm, all the while dig into the bare forearm with your fingers. Search for the eyes. When your partner feels his eyes have been attacked, he may let loose. You may escape and take appropriate action. I have done this successfully in real life and multiple times in very hard core training sessions. Surviving the ground eye attack is my litmus test. I do not teach ground fighting tactics that may be easily defeated by an opponent's eye attacks. This removes about 50 percent or more of all submission fighting, sport judo and wrestling based tactics.

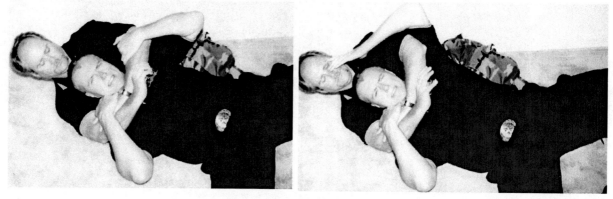

CS 5: Hand Counters Eye Jab – A Sample Study

The enemy eye jabs at you with an open fingers thrust attack.

He attacks!   *You reflexively raise your hand.*

You block and feel that your fingers have accidentally intertwined.

You viciously rip and twist the fingers you caught. Quick! Vicious!

Finish as morally, ethically or legally needed. Here we brought the head to the knee with a palm strike to the face.

Your Finger Strike Module Review and Assignment

Practice the different finger attacks:

Open finger *rake* strikes

Closed finger *spear* strikes

Hooking finger attack to the eye

Thrusting fingers attack to the eye

Pinching fingers

One (or both) thumb gouge

Finger slap to the nose

Grappling finger fish hook

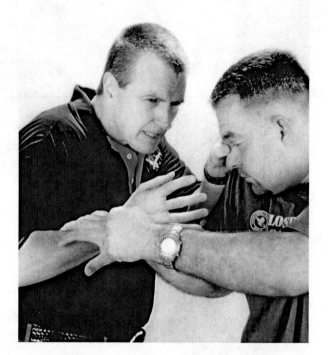

Work finger attack synergy drills:

Solo command and mastery in the air
— use the clock drill format.

Solo command and mastery hitting devices for power
— use flashing focus mitts.
— use heavy bags.

Partner Drills
Statue Drill and Pumping Drill
— outside, inside, inside, outside format

Flow drills walking, standing, kneeling and on the ground
— use the block, pass and pin drill. Develop inserts.

Ground roll drill, with eye attack inserts

Clinch drill, with eye attack inserts.

Practice combat scenarios standing, kneeling and on the ground.

Use both offensive and defensive problem situations.

Unarmed Combatives Kick Module 1)
The Frontal Snapping Kick Module

The front snap kick begins with a snapping motion from the knee joint with synchronized help from the hip joint and proper body support balance. It uses the tip of a shoed foot, the top of the foot, the shin up to the knee as a striking surface. Using the ball of the foot is not practical in shoes. This kick is often used in close quarter combat when the enemy is not in some type of martial fighting stance. This will be demonstrated in the following combat scenarios. In face-off, sparring situations, the front snap kick is often used as a setup or stall. The fact that the opponent is standing somewhat sideways limits the effect of the kick. Many use this kick wisely as simply a shoe tip to the shin.

FSK Studies and Observations 1) Balance
Much training effort and detail is directed to the leg that actually strikes. Remember the other leg. The springy bend of the standing knee, the direction of the standing foot. Each kick is a double leg study to create balance. Every time you lift your leg to kick, you challenge your balance in close quarter combat.

FSK Studies and Observations 2) Chambering
Many martial artists obsess about chambering the kick and punch. Chambering is typically rearing your strike back and then firing it forward, under the assumption that it gains more power with this process. Does it? I believe if it were scientifically measured, we would be debating a micro-second and few ounces of a per-pound-strike ratio. I also believe that there is a point of retraction where a chamber delivers a maximum result and that special point might not be a full, folded, classical chamber. Find a point in your own experimentation where you get maximum results with minimum movement. Isn't that the true tenet of modern fighting? In the case of a frontal snap kick, many chamber their leg by raising their knee first and snapping their lower leg for the kick.

Front Snap Kick Synergy Drills

Solo Command and Mastery Drill
1) Frontal Snap Kick: Shuffle
Lead Foot Delivery

The shuffle foot is when your rear foot shuffles up near your front foot. You attempt to square off your hips and then your front leg fires a snapping motion. Hands remain up in the window of combat.

You shuffle your rear foot near the lead foot, then kick with your lead leg. You must sync up these motions for balance and power.

You can rest all your weight back on the rear leg and then quickly snap the lead leg up for a kick. You must sync up these motions to have balance and power.

From a fight position, you lean back with most of your weight on your rear leg and deliver a frontal snapping kick with your free front leg. Note the black mark reference point on the floor for foot positioning.

Solo Command and Mastery Frontal Snap Kick 2) The Rear Leg Frontal Snapping Kick Delivery

You may try to square up your hips as you swing your rear leg through for the kick.

Note the black mark on the floor for foot position reference.

Solo Command and Mastery 3) Frontal Snap Kick from Your Back Delivery

For every kick you practice standing, you must also exercise from ground positions.

Solo Command and Mastery Frontal Snap Kick 4) Ground Side Delivery
From your back turn to your side and deliver a frontal kick with the top of your leg.

Note: We do not usually front snap kick with the bottom-side leg due to lack of mobility and power. Experiment with it, if you wish. I do not mandate it.

Drill 2) Counters to the Front Snap Kick

There are various early, mid and late phase counters to the kick. These counters will be explored heavily in the following combat scenarios. The basic counters are executed in the three phases: early-phase, mid-phase and late-phase.

Counter 1) Evasion

Counter 2) Kick the kick

Counter 3) Swallow the kick

Counter 4) Catch the kick

Counter 5) Deal with the pain

Kick the kick is shown above on the left as an oblique kick in an early phase counter to a front snap kick. On the right is a simple retraction evasion.

Frontal Snap Kick Partner Synergy Drills

Work through these kicks the following three ways: Execute in the air. Then kick a shield or kicking mitt. A partner should hold a mitt or pad about groin high. Next, a partner flashes the mitt in a sparring environment to develop speed.

FSK Drill 1) 10 kicks from each leg of a neutral or natural stance

The natural stance is a non-fighting position, or how you might normally stand on a street corner and suddenly be attacked. You will stand in this normal position. After each neutral kick, return to a fighting/ready stance. Then position yourself back into the neutral stance to begin practice again.

Neutral Stance Kicking 1) Execute 10 kicks right leg.
   – in the air
   – against a pad

Neutral Stance Kicking 2) Execute 10 kicks left leg.
   – in the air
   – against a pad

FSK Drill 2) 20 kicks from the front leg of an aggressive stance. A microsecond before the kick, move your hand or shoulder to distract the enemy. If you always practice in this manner, you will reflexively have a fake built into each kick.

The neutral/natural stance.

Each time you kick, fake first, then kick. Make the fake an important part of each kick.

Aggressive Stance Kicking) 10 kicks, lead right leg
Aggressive Stance Kicking) 10 kicks, lead left leg
Thailand-Style Kicking Set) 9 kicks, rapid fire, sets of 3 each

FSK Drill 3) 20 kicks from the rear leg of a fighting stance

Aggressive Stance Kicking) 10 kicks, rear leg right
Aggressive Stance Kicking) 10 kicks, rear leg left

FSK Drill 4) 20 kicks from the Combat Modified FSK. Your lead foot, knee and hip are turned in varying degrees enough to strike around the lead leg of an enemy's fighting stance, yet still maintaining the basic frontal snap kick motion.

Aggressive Stance Kicking) 10 modified right lead leg kicks
Aggressive Stance Kicking) 10 modified left lead leg leads

FSK Drill 5) 40 kicks grounded

Grounded) 10 kicks on your back, kick left leg
Grounded) 10 kicks on your back kick right leg
Grounded) 10 kicks on your right side with your left leg
Grounded) 10 kicks on your left side with your right leg

Kicking from your back

FSK Give and Take Drill
In four kicks, in two per partner, exchange kicks. Deal with this exchange in the following sets:

Set 1) Evasion – get away from the impact.
Set 2) Tap the kick – evade and tap it with your hand if it comes in high enough.
Set 3) Kick the kick, as in a stop kick or re-direction.

Frontal Snap Kick Option Awareness Combat Scenarios

Practice these combat scenarios. They offer great variety in attacking and countering the FSK.

CS 1) Kick the Choker – A Sample Study
The enemy grabs your throat in the common street fight two-handed choke.

You are attacked. You attack the eyes. You front snap kick the groin.

Push the head down. You elbow strike the back of the neck.
You forearm bash the back of the neck.

CS 2) Kick the Encroacher – A Sample Study

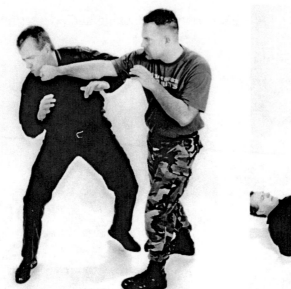

You have been knocked down on your back. The enemy walks up to finish the fight. You maneuver into a position where you may gain access to a groin kick. You lift your body up to front snap kick his groin.

Execute a pushing/pulling leg attack as shown. Once the enemy is down, kick vital targets as available.

CS 3) Vise Grip the Kicker: A Sample Study

The enemy lands a successful kick to your groin. You reflexively vise grip your legs before he snaps away. You turn your body so both of you face the same direction.

DIVE! You dive chest down taking him down with you. After you do this several times, you learn what direction to dive that best produce the enemy's face down fall.

You spin and wrench his knee. Take your right fist, in this case, and execute a head or neck hammer fist strike.

Hopefully, the body crash, knee wrench and hammer fist will buy a few stunned seconds. If so? Next, get up on all fours. With a posted hand on his back, fire multiple knee strikes to the groin and body. Then climb up. Make the climb pin and hurt.

Kick the head. Note my left leg is over his lower right leg in an effort to control or feel his movement. Get up and take out optional targets. Avoid wrestling in real world encounters, if at all possible. There are many optional follow-ups to engage in after the initial dive. Experiment and explore other options.

CS 4) Knock-Knee the Kick: A Sample Study

This bent-in knee is an old martial arts tactic that protects the groin.

The enemy kicks at your groin. You see it coming and try for this early phase counter.

This is from his view. You turn your hip and bring knees together, as shown in this first step to block and/or deflect the kick.

Make sure the block sticks. You clear his arms and punch the enemy's throat. If this doesn't bang him away, continue the counter-attack. You finish the fight as appropriate.

CS 5) Down On All Fours Kick Counter Series: Sample Studies

In this series of four scenarios, you have been downed on all fours and the enemy approaches you and attacks you from all four sides: the top, bottom, right and left. In Combat Scenario 5A he kicks you in the side. In 5B you are down and he tries to kick you in the face. Both are very common street attacks.

CS 5A - FSK coming in from either the right or left side

You are hit! Down you drop. As any typical thug might attack you, here the enemy tries to kick you in the ribs. You prepare yourself for the impact. Exhale. Lift your torso on impact.

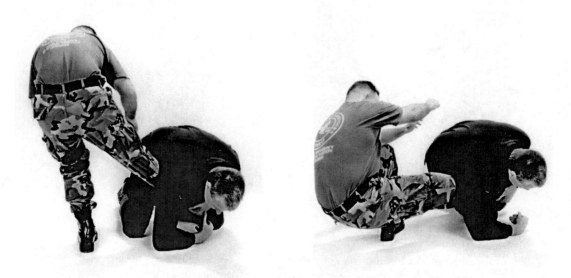

Catch the leg and roll against the shin.

Hope he takes the surprise fall hard and perhaps bangs his head on the floor. Make the first counter strike an elbow to the groin as you smother the leg. Knock and/or push the other leg out of the way if need be.

Start the roll for the next strike. You might select another elbow strike to the sternum, then roll up to yet another elbow strike to the face. (A lot depends on the width of your body. Will a revolution turn you too far and make you miss an intended target?)

You could target the sternum with a powerful, bone breaking knee strike. Lift the leg high and crash down. A slight hop toward the head could produce another knee to the face.

CS 5B - FSK Coming into Your Face, or Topside Attack

You have been knocked down. The enemy comes to front snap kick you in the face.
You use your forearms to both block and capture the blow.

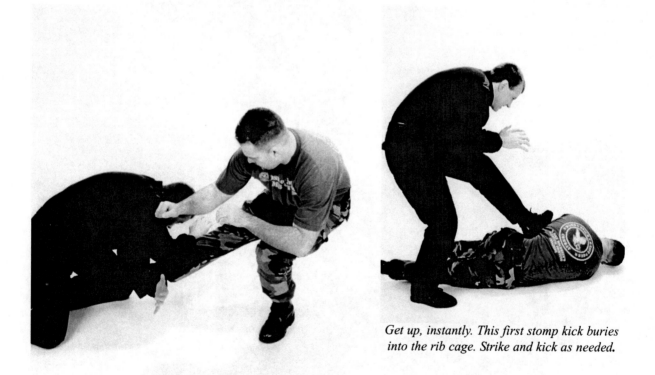

Get up, instantly. This first stomp kick buries into the rib cage. Strike and kick as needed.

With this leg wrap you execute a push/pull style takedown.

CS 6) Standing Counter Kick: The Arm-Catch Series: Sample Studies

In this series, you are standing and attacked by the FSK. You dodge the force of a real front snap kick and its unstopped energy can take the kick higher than the groin, the usual intended target. It is important to remember that when any deliberate enemy with a mission tries to injure you with this snap kick, it is usually delivered with a great deal of angry energy. If he or she misses the target, this kick will usually fly up higher than planned. Here is where we hope to take advantage of this mistake and snatch the leg.

The angry, missed snap kick often travels higher than planned!

Kick Catching Overview

There are four sets of basic arm catches. These foundation movements can also catch thrust, side and round kicks. Remember them throughout this **CQCG** course. Here are the four solo practice catching movements.

Catch Series 1) Same-side uppercut catch.

Catch Series 2) Same-side arm down catch.

Catch Series 3) Cross-body uppercut (right to left side and vice-versa).

Hybrid Catch Series 4) Your hands catch the clothing of the leg or the leg itself.

Note: Passing - Passing a kick is also a counter tactic, shown here on the ground.

In the course of a fight you may wind up in this position. The enemy kicks at you. You see it coming and reflexively block. It hurts, but you minimize the attack by taking it in the forearm rather than your head. Then you go with the momentum.

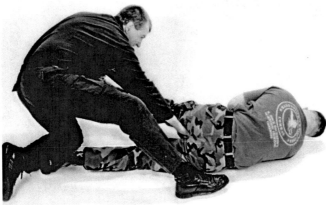

"If you can't catch it? Pass it!" This is an excellent rule of combat.

Duck and pass the energy. Destroy any targets available with strikes and kicks. Here a power punch to the groin is delivered.

CS 6A) Go Forward: Arm catches the kick and pitches forward with a run. The power kick misses, and the leg comes high. You uppercut catch and run forward.

If you laid the training clock down on the floor, this forward direction would be to your 12 o'clock takedown.

CS 6B) Go Right – A Sample
You catch the missed kick, roll it over and take him down. Smash the knee into the ground.

He kicks hard and misses. You catch and turn right.

*Run and push his leg into
a bend and crash him
off balance.*

Use the knee to steer.

Lift and smash the kneecap.

If you laid the training clock down on the floor, this forward direction would be to your 9 o'clock takedown.

CS 6C) Go Back – A Sample

This time you make a scooping catch, then a turnaround and run. Note, the arm switch to turn and maintain the catch. Quick and devastating.

If you laid the training clock down on the floor, this forward direction would be to your 6 o'clock takedown.

CS 6D) Go Left – A Sample Study

You scoop/catch and turn to your left. Violently strike the face (shown here as eye jab), then perform the classic rear takedown.

If you laid the training clock down on the floor, this forward direction would be to your 3 o'clock takedown.

Your Frontal Snapping Kick Module Review and Assignment

Practice the 5 different frontal snapping kicks:
In the air and against pads and shields

FSK 1) Front leg frontal snapping kicks

FSK 2) Rear leg frontal snapping kicks

FSK 3) Combat modified frontal snapping kicks

FSK 4) On your back frontal snapping kicks

FSK 5) On your right side and left side kicks

Practice the 4 Count Give and Take Frontal Snapping Kicking Drill

FSK Drill Set 1) Body and leg evasion

FSK Drill Set 2) Tap and/or feel the incoming kick

FSK Drill Set 3) Kick the kick. Stop kick it or deflect it

Practice combat scenarios standing, kneeling and on the ground.
Use both offensive and defensive problem situations.

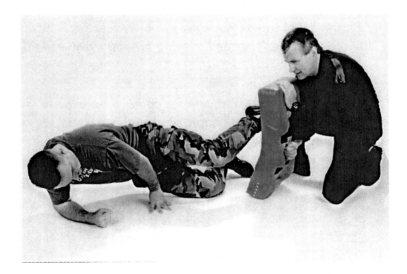

CQC Group

UC Invading Hands 1: The Outside Arm or The Backhand Contact Strike

Invading Hands is a term used in our CQC Group meaning arm-to-arm attack methods to get into extreme close quarter combat range. Some martial arts practitioners call them *trapping* hands and make an obsessive study of the subject, often at the expense of practice in other important combat ranges. The so-called trapping range between two antagonists is really those few inches in which you or he pass in a micro-second charge to escalate the fight. It is an extremely short, transitory range. Mobility is king. When we look at the hard science, here are the principles.

The Definition
Invading hands is the immobilization, deflection and/or control of the opponent's limbs with one clear mission, to clear a path to a vital target, usually the face, neck or groin. This is done by the four P's, pinning, passing, pulling, pushing that grabs that freezes or steers the enemy limbs. Invading hands is absolutely nothing more than simply getting the arms of the enemy out of your way. It is that simple. You want to strike a better target, and the guy's arms are in the way.

The Obstructions
His arms are usually raised up in a variety of aggressive or defensive positions, and the body is usually, or becomes, naturally bladed from you.

Obstruction 1 – The closest, lead arm
Obstruction 2 – The second arm
Obstruction 3 – The lead arm manages to come around again and get in the way.

In a perfect invasion, you will only deal with one, two invasions, three at the most. If his arms are still up after four or more times? Kick the knee. Or regroup yourself for another plan. If you are invading in close with your legs and striking properly, you should get results.

The Meeting of the Minds...and Arms
The meeting of your arm with his arm is best called a *contact,* because it could be from either an aggressive attack or defensive block. Some people refer to these contact spots as reference points to organize their training practice. This contact is done whether he has struck out at you, or you take a pre-emptive strike back at him. A block alone is just a block, a reflex contact without counter-attack. A block with strike is an invading hand. These reference points could be with arms high or arms low.

The level one study is the backhanded contact. I use the terms *backhand* or *outside arm* as they are easily recognized by everyone. It actually suggests the backside of your fingers, hand, forearm and upper arm, and this includes from the edges of your forearms to the so-called knife edge, or sides of your hand.

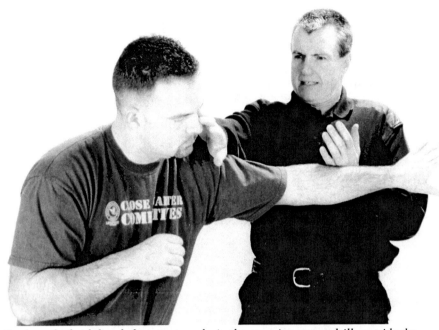

See how the back-handed contact works in the pumping statue drill, outside the enemy's arms. You use the outside of your arm.

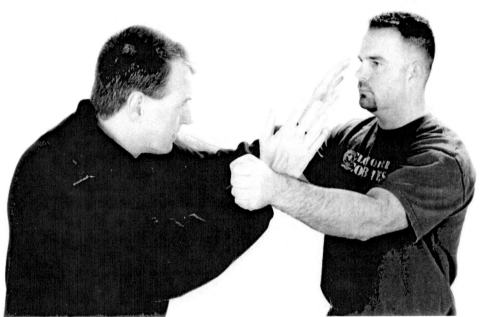

See how the back-handed contact works in the statue drill inside the enemy's arms. You use the outside of your arm.

The Strikes

You invade and trap the arms with powerful palm strikes, hammer fists and forearms, forceful enough to break bricks! You strike your targets with eye jabs, thrusting and hooking palm strikes, fists, forearm, elbows and body rams. Kicking may be involved and there are leg invasions as well, studied in later levels.

The Training

There is a good reason the prior invading hands photos look a lot like some of the Finger Strike Module photos. In this level, the Invading Hand module resembles the very same steps we studied in the finger strike module. In the finger strike workout we had to clear a path to get the strike in. That path-clearing method? That was this very invading hand method. That is why I collected the two methods together here for *Mission One.* The set-up for the strike was an obstruction-clearing invasion. When training and teaching in this Invasion Hand Module, you repeat the same drills and steps as in the Finger Strike Module, except you emphasize and notice the invasion aspects. The strike could be a finger attack, or any attack.

When I instruct CQC Group or Unarmed Combatives Level One, I include the Finger Strike Module in with the Invasion Hand Module, explain the similarities. In later levels there are no such similarities between the hand strikes and invading hand tactics.

Try using hand weights that have the support handle, the bar that allows a person to slip their hands inside and open their hands when needed. Usually reserved for runners, these hand weights develop hand strikes and therefore constitute a goal-specific exercise. These hand weights also are excellent and legal brass knuckles to leave laying around your car or home for self defense purposes.

Your Backhand Module Review and Assignment

Practice the movements in the air.
Practice the movements against training equipment with a simulated, extended arm.
Practice the Statue Drill - using the motions versus a person with their arms extended.
Practice the Pumping Drill - using the motions versus a person punching their arms.
Practice the movements inside the Block, Pass and Pin Synergy Drill.
Practice these motions in combat scenarios on standing, kneeling and ground positions.

CQC Group

Unarmed Combatives Takedown 1:
The Finger Takedowns Module

Finger Takedowns Overview
One of the most powerful and efficient tools in fighting are finger cranks and eventual finger breaks if necessary. The study of finger cranks, breaks and takedowns is a blended endeavor for this CQCG Level 1 and it works in conjunction with the use of finger strikes as a theme progression. Finger cranks rarely are a simple end to a fight, but rather a means to an end. After a stunning blow to an attacker, they can have a strong influence when transitioned into escapes from grabs, takedowns and throws. The fingers are thin bones and unnatural manipulation of them may cause great pain, shock, even within some of the highest levels of adrenaline pumping through an enemy. The visual shock of someone seeing their own finger broken and askew may cause a significant, sudden distraction and increase the shock factor. Finger cranks may be direct links to the manipulation of the wrist, the arm and then body.

It is important that you know you cannot stand before a raging wildman and attempt to snatch his finger when he charges at you. The finger crank comes after he grabs you in some manner, and with proper stunning and diminishment, you get a finger or two of the grab. In 30 years of police work and martial arts training, usually people react severely to having their fingers cranked.

Finger Takedowns Studies and Observations 1) Cranks of 10 Fingers
Each of the 10 fingers bend in five directions:

> Bend 1 – all the way in
> Bend 2 – all the way back (probably gives you the best results)
> Bend 3 – side-to-side
> Bend 4 – twisting in
> Bend 5 – twisting out

Finger Takedowns, Studies and Observations 2) The Thumb's Range of Motion
The thumb may also be cranked, but it is meatier and more deeply attached to the hand than the fingers. Working on the thumb is much like working on a bridge to the wrist. The thumb may be efficiently bent only four ways due to the positioning on the hand.

Finger Takedowns, Studies and Observations 3) The Finger Squeeze
Sometimes the individual joints of a finger may be squeezed together to create pain.

Finger Takedowns, Studies and Observations 4) How Many Fingers?
Four fingers grabbed and cranked together can offer resistance. Three? Better. Two or one may be the weakest and best number. One finger might slink free. Two may not escape so easily.

Finger Takedowns Studies and Observations
5) Handcuffing
Finger cranks may be especially effective in the last steps in manipulating a prisoner of war, or a criminal, into handcuffs or other ligatures, something I have experienced hundreds and hundreds of times. We study more of these manipulations in the Control and Contain Module in *CQCG Training Mission Three.*

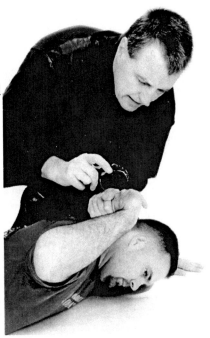

The Finger Crank Synergy Drills

FC Drill 1) Block, Pass and Pin Drill
Using the block, pass and pin drill detailed earlier in this book, try to obtain some finger snatches and cranks. On Step/Beat 1 1/2 of the drill, catch the fingers from behind and peel backward for pain and a takedown as demonstrated in this series.

In this series, the trainee blocks on Step/Beat 1, a very common, instinctive movement. This is against an open handed slap or eye jab — the subject matter of this level. Of course if this were a punch, the fingers would not be open and available for this attack.

IT IS JUST A SKILL DRILL!

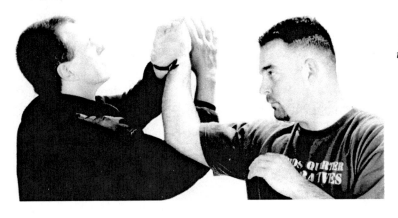

On Step/Beat 1 1/2 the trainee hooks under the stopped, attacking arm, and gets a grip on some of the fingers.

Next, the trainee gets both his hands on the captured hand and fingers. Twist the fingers and wrist violently outward and downward, all the while stepping to the outside.

FC Drill 2) Finger Attack Ground Roll Drill for Escapes

Finger cranks may interrupt the best of ground attacks. Experiment with catching the fingers during free style ground fighting. When the enemy grabs you, his fingers are on you, and they may be subject to a finger crank, dislocation or break. At varying levels of intensity, do some wrestling and see what finger cranks become available. Use a coach with each team of two practitioners because new trainees tend to miss many obvious opportunities.

The biggest training problem with this endeavor is new participants to the drill will finger chase and not realistically fight on the ground. You seize the finger when it incidentally and accidentally happens to be catchable. Coaches need to be aware of this recurring problem. Coaches also need to be specifically aware of trained submission fighters. They will routinely completely forget the finger attack opportunity. They must be interrupted and reminded that the finger crank is their objective in this drill.

All ground fighting practice should be overseen by a competent and street-fight enlightened coach to guide the participants into maximizing their survival. Too often, ground fighters cannot see options because their vision is blocked by the closeness of the other fighter.

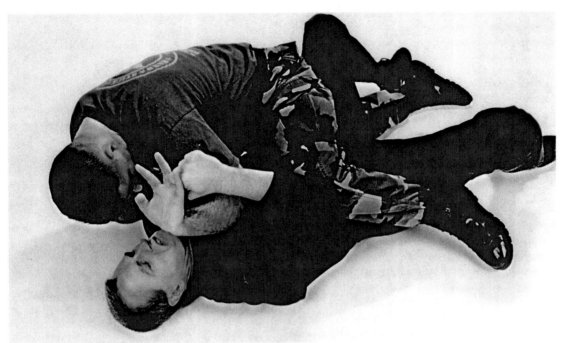

If you are trained to be aware, the enemy's hands fall into your range constantly during ground combat. A crank or break may have a major negative effect on the opponent.

Finger Takedown Option Awareness Combat Scenarios

Here are some sample combat scenarios using finger cranks and finger related takedowns.

FT CS 1) Counter a Single Grab on Arm – A Sample Study

This is a control-attempt grab by an enemy, with limited intimidation and threat, and not an attack done in full-blown, madman, extreme combat boxing ring conditions.

The common first-conflict grab. Is it a simple grab or a set-up for a punch?

A fist across the carotid could shut the attack down, or at least post-pone it for a few stunned seconds. You could try to yank your arm out of the grab! Or, as shown to the right, if you finger grab the stunned opponent, it may quickly get him down.

It worked! He is down. This may signal the end of the conflict. But if not? Switch hands (the new grip does not have to include the previously caught finger) and bash the jaw line and neck area again. Bash as needed.

The finger crank may peel you free from the common grabs of a newly stunned opponent. If you can hang on to that finger or maybe two a bit longer, you may be able to put the assailant down and then out. The crank is inside an overall counter-attack of many parts.

FT CS 2) Counter a Double Grab – A Sample Study

The enemy grabs the sides of your forearms. This time your forearm is down near your side. This is another look at a hostile grab, not a full-blown, madman, boxing style attack.

The grab.

This time a front kick – the subject kick of this level – into the groin.

One hand reaches under...

...and grabs the ball of the thumb of the far hand.

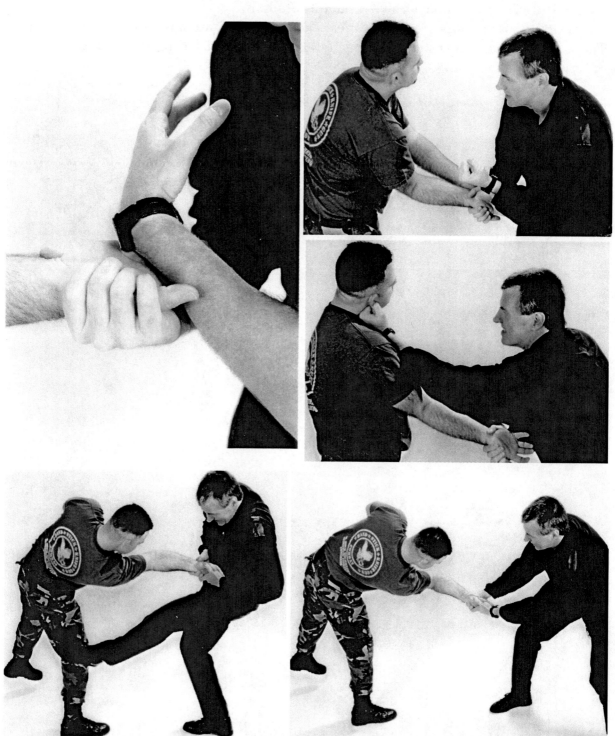

There is a subtle, chopping thumb attack available if you have time, in the split second shown in the upper left corner photo. As soon as your hand gets free, in a straight, efficient line, blast the throat. Blast more if needed. To explore our finger attack to the thumb, then return to the fore-arm and thumb/wrist twisting process. Kick the knee, if needed. Step around his right side and pull down. Remember, any kind of wrist crank is always harder than you expect. The only way you will learn this is through experimentation.

FT CS 3) Finger Crank Counters a Rear Bear Hug – A Sample Study

This is a control grab of intimidation and threat, and not one done in extreme combat conditions. This is a classic scenario that requires experimentation.

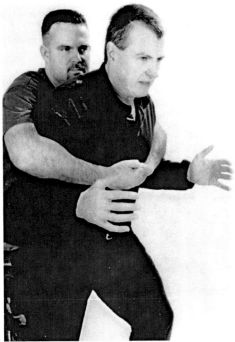

The criminal grabs you.

You snap kick the groin or shin kick.
Multiple kicks are fine. Kick as needed.

You step back and hopefully pull the enemy off balance. Pound the back of his
hands with your knuckles, targeting those frail bones. This really hurts!
Done fiercely enough, you may escape right here.

Crank that finger back and use all your body weight to turn out of the now-open hold.

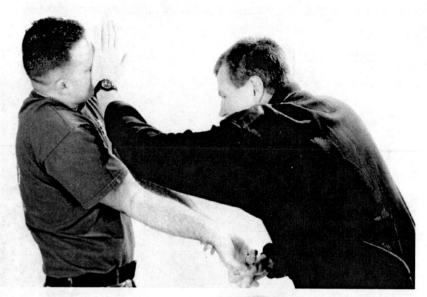

Strike as soon as possible and as many times as needed.

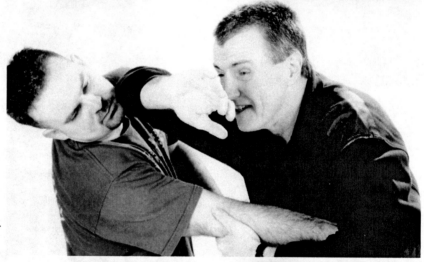

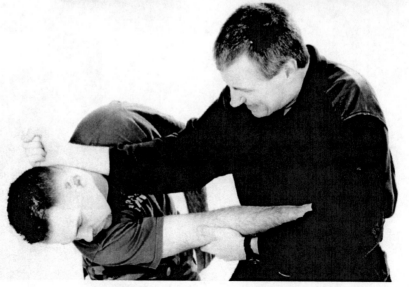

FT CS 4) Counter the Double Hand Choke – A Sample Study

This is one of the most common, angry assaults. There are many possible responses. This one exercises the finger crank because it is the subject of our study.

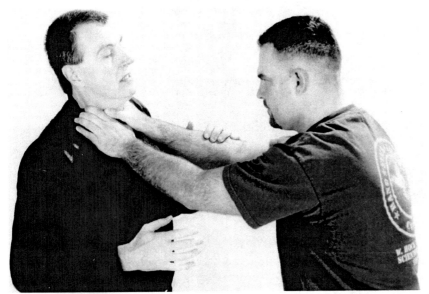

The common street choke.

Throat strike! You must stun first. Strike again as needed. This may end the attack right here.

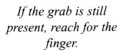

If the grab is still present, reach for the finger.

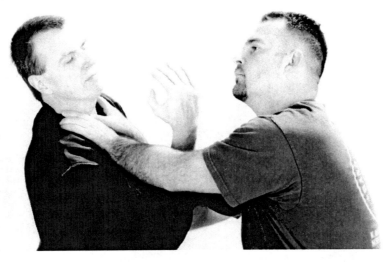

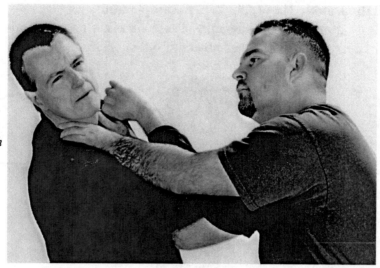

Crank the finger back against the knuckle. Use your other hand to control his elbow. Rip down from the high left to the low right.

Get him off of you, down, and them bash him out.

FT CS 6) Counter a Double-Handed Push: The *Two Six-Guns Crank* – A Sample Study

A bully enemy starts to shove you to provoke or intimidate you. This is not a full blown, mad-man fistfight. But it could become one. This tactic has good potential vs. a pushing bully.

He pushes you once and gets away with it. He pushes twice. Your fingers accidentally begin to intertwine.

You take quick advantage of this accident. You do not ram your fingers against his to go web-to-web deep. Keep some distance from the web and start to turn you hands outward.

This is the ultimate positioning of your fingers upon his fingers. It will take some experience and perhaps some coaching to get it. Once you do, you will be able to achieve this quick capture a majority of the time.

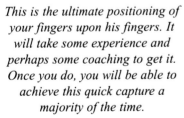

Here is an isolated and solo look at the hand and finger positioning. You turn palms upward and crank down. Hold your hands as though you are gripping two large jar lids, or two revolvers. Practice rotating and also turning your hands inward as though you are taking off the lids. Then add a painful snapping like you are firing bullets out of the pistols.

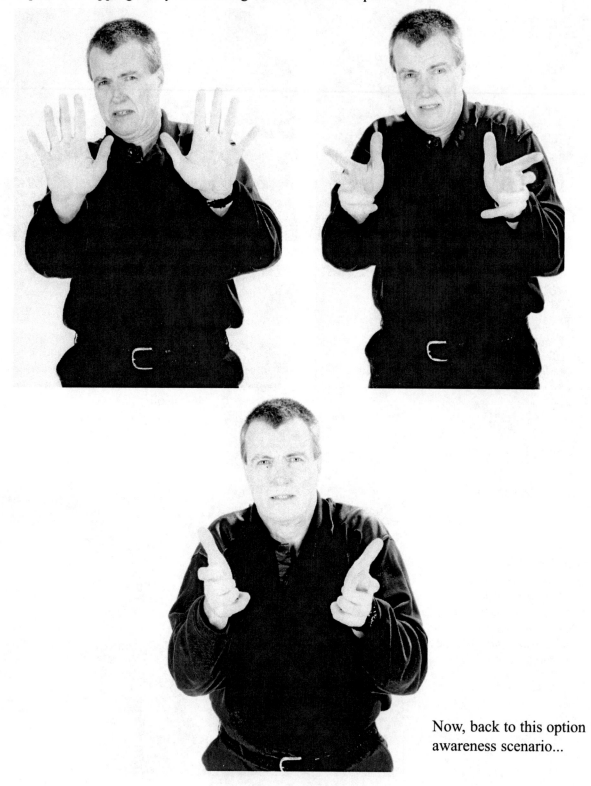

Now, back to this option awareness scenario...

Try to whip the hands into the slanted six gun position as previously shown. Fire a "few rounds" by cranking your wrists forward one wrist at a time. This usually hurts.

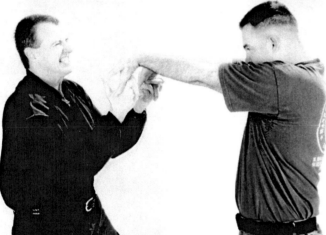

This is the perfect position. If you can get the bully up on his toes doing the "Ballerina," you have the move. Take note of the position of the arms.

Scientifically, you can move him down to the right, to the left and if the height is correct, over the head for takedowns. Lead with his palms.

Don't try to tell me this can't be done in real life. I have done this as an arresting officer with a resisting felon who pushed me away twice. The second time, I accidentally twined his fingers and, thanks to training, realized a possibility. I did what is shown here. The man squealed all the way down. This movement can also be done with one hand catching one hand.

FT CS 7) Counter to a Pistol Threat – A Sample Study

An entire volume could be written about the psychologies of this moment. Those psychologies will appear in great detail in the weapon disarm module in *CQCG Training Mission Four.* Here we are only investigating the mechanics as they relate to attacking the enemy's finger. The enemy presents a pistol in close range. This is a common, criminal presentation.

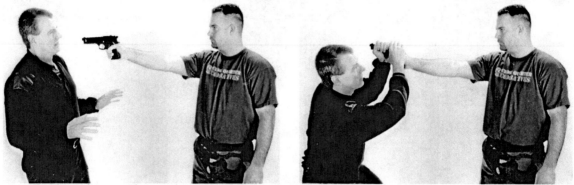

The threat begins. The pistol is within lunge and reach. You raise your hands in the ruse of surrender. Without staring at the pistol, you grab for it. Clear the barrel. Get both hands on the pistol. This can render it a one-shot, or no shot weapon. More on this in future books.

Crank the pistol directly over the back of the hand. Capture the trigger finger inside the trigger guard.

Here is a clear photo of the finger trapped inside the guard. You either dislocate or break the finger as you rip the pistol down. Bash the neck as soon as possible. Remember, when confiscating the firearm of another, you do not know if it will function.

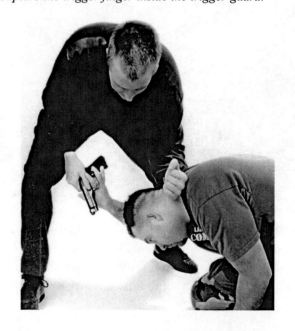

Counters and Escapes to Finger Cranks and Takedowns

There are basic countering times that apply to almost all tactics in the process of being applied on you: things you may do early on, things you may try in the middle, and things you attempt late in the application.

> Early-Phase Counters – when the attack tactic first begins
> Mid-Phase Counters – when the attack tactic is near the middle of formation
> Late-Phase Counters – when the attack tactic is near completion

As with hardening cement, the escapes usually become harder to achieve as the tactic unfolds. The general countering and escape tactics that foul locks/cranks joint related takedowns and throws are:

> Countering and Escape 1) Explosive retraction in an early phase
> Countering and Escape 2) Striking the attacker in mid to late phase
> Countering and Escape 3) Kicking the attacker in the three phases
>
> Countering and Escape 4) Going limp.
> Much pain originates in the struggle and resistance that you put into fighting the joint lock/attack. There are several joint attacks that can be countered by going loose and limp.
>
> Countering and Escape 5) Going to the ground ahead of the tactic.
> When caught in this late phase, go where YOU want to go on the ground, not where he plans to put you. Move ahead of the takedown to maximize your next position.
>
> Countering and Escape 6) Hybrid problem.
> There are some solutions that are unique to that particular attack.
>
> Countering and Escape 7) Pain Tolerance.
> On the battlefield there is no tap-out. Some 60 percent of the grappling tactics taught to bring on a sport tap-out surrender, may be fought through with experience, knowledge and pain tolerance.

A counter is used when the opponent has not completed his tactic in swift, split second efficiency. Being human, odds are in your favor the opponent will not be able to attack perfectly due to his foibles, his condition, clothing, even the weather! The chaos! This problem goes for you too! That is why you must study many options. This subject matter will be presented in a complete thesis summation, as will all major fighting topics in *CQCG Training Mission Ten*. We will proceed here outlining only the counters that relate to finger crank attacks and takedowns.

Early phase counter. He gets you, but not quite yet in a tight grip. You explode out. A common drunk or an untrained child will simply yank back to escape an unwanted grab.

Counter and Escape – The explosive retraction in an early phase of attack.

He grabs you. Before the grab hardens, you explode free. This is sheer instinct.

Counter and Escape – The impact/slap release in an early phase of attack.

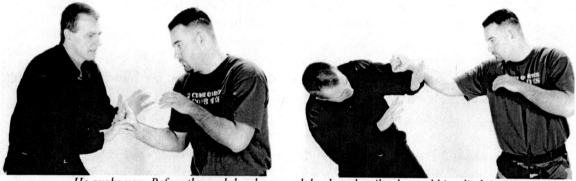

He grabs you. Before the grab hardens, yank back and strike the grabbing limb in
a push/pull type of movement. The push/pull must fit the angle of the capture.

Counter and Escape – Striking the attacker
in any phase possible.

Counter and Escape – Kick the attacker
in any phase possible.

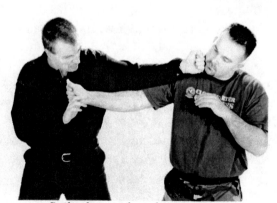

Strike the attacker when possible.

Kick the legs of the opponent whenever possible.

Counter and Escape – Going to the ground.

Here we escape in the late phase. The trainer is about to put the trainee down on his chest for further destruction. Knowing this, the trainee interrupts the plan. Falling where he chooses, he drops instead onto his back and kicks.

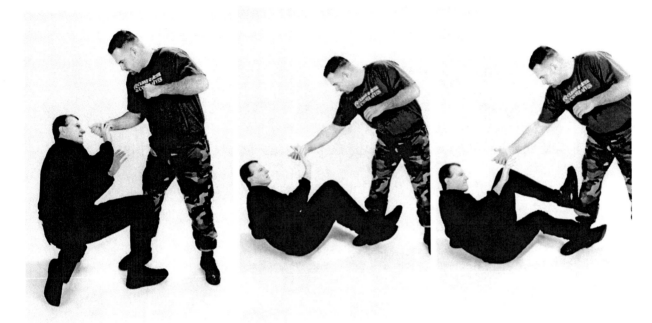

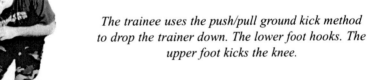

The trainee uses the push/pull ground kick method to drop the trainer down. The lower foot hooks. The upper foot kicks the knee.

Continue the kicking assault. Next, the trainee targets the groin with his right leg. Note the position of his left leg, temporarily in the way of the opponent's right leg kick. The science of street ground fighting includes far more of these types of strategies than simply wrestling.

Finger Crank Takedown Summary

Very simply put, after you have been grabbed, you stun an opponent, get a finger or some of the fingers grabbing you and crank the fire out of them. You may have to break them in some dire circumstances. Escape the grab, or if you hang on to the fingers a second or two longer, you may see an opportunity to use the fingers as a takedown tactic.

Your Finger Crank Takedown Module Review and Assignment

Practice the Skill Drill

Block, Pass and Pin Drill – Catch the fingers on the half beats of the drill.

The Ground Roll Drill – Catch the fingers for escapes during the drill.

Practice Finger Crank Takedowns Combat Scenarios

Do both preemptive offensive scenarios and defensive scenarios.

Do the counter pistol threat scenario.

Practice Countering the Finger Crank Takedowns

Do combat scenarios countering the finger cranks.

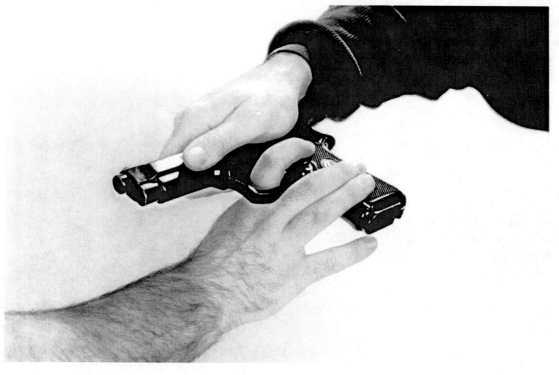

CQC Group

Gun/Counter-Gun Combatives 1
Pistol and Long Gun Quick Draws

Introduction to Weaponry:
The Quick Draw Imperative

We have completed our study of the Level One Unarmed Combatives material, and now we begin the requirements concerning modern weapons. The very first combat step in using a pistol, a knife, impact weapon and/or a long gun is its first acquisition – its quick draw. This vital, primary step is overlooked by most training systems that instead opt to train with the weapon, already magically having appeared in one's hand. Pulling that weapon under combat stress is an important skill.

The Level One knife, stick and gun courses deal with quick draws under combat stress, when the action really begins. I ask you here to pay special heed to the segments on pistol quick draws because the basic principles often directly apply to the quick draw of the knife and impact weapon as well.

Studies and Observations 1) Gun/Counter – Gun Fighting Body of Knowledge
There exists only a very small body of mechanical knowledge about the operation of pistol and long gun shooting. One may cull through years of the many popular gun manuals, books and magazines on the market and see the same information rerun dozens and dozens of times.

The Three Mechanical Layers of Working the Gun
Fundamental pistol and long gun shooting simply includes:

> Layer 1) Knowledge of the weapon function.

> Layer 2) Knowledge of the ammo.

> Layer 3) Knowledge and skill of marksmanship mechanics.

Knowledge of Safety Rules
The basic body of knowledge contains a few general rules of safety. Each shooting academy has its own rules of safety list. The lists vary from a very basic few to over 15. The universal main four usually go as follows:

> Safety Rule 1) All guns are loaded.

> Safety Rule 2) Never point one unless you have a need to destroy and are committed to destroy.

> Safety Rule 3) Finger off the trigger until shooting.

> Safety Rule 4) Be sure of your target and beyond.

The Million Layers of Gun Combat
Combat gun and counter-gun fighting requires much more than mechanical function. In fact, there are a million layers, as the following essay endeavors to explain. First, think of the differences between these statements.

> Running on a treadmill. Running a marathon in the woods.

> Weight lifting in a gym. Carrying logs down the side of mountain in the rain.

> Playing catch with a football. Being in a pro football game.

Just a few stark differences between the training method and the end goal, performance? The treadmill and the gym can help prepare you to do these tasks, but the tasks themselves are inside many layers of diverse and adverse conditions and distractions.

Remember your very first driving lesson? You learned how far to turn the steering wheel before the car responded. How the brakes worked! How soft pedal pressure moved the half-ton monster. Getting down the first empty street was a big adventure. Backing up between the cones a challenge.

Now look at you! Whipping through Manhattan, L.A., Atlanta or Dallas. A million cars whizzing around. Cell phones broadcasting. A burger and fries on your lap. You are daydreaming and jamming with the radio. Your kids may be fighting in the back seat. After day care, you have a million chores to do, the bank, post office. Laundry. Traffic jams. Jerks. Rain and slick roads. Pedestrians! Politics on the job. India and Pakistan with nukes! There are a million physical and mental layers involved with driving that car in and through the terrain of your life. That 15-year-old you were once, the teen that slid pristine behind the wheel learned only the first thin layer of driving in the real world…

> *This is the brake.*
> *This is the horn.*
> *This is the seat belt.*
> *This is a right turn.*
> *This is how you park.*
> *Now get ready for the million layers of driving.*

The million layers? They are the things that happen in and around you while driving. Learning the mechanics of operating a car and driving today's streets are vastly different. No, this is not a driver's safety lecture.This is a message from the bloody clearinghouse of gunfights. Going to the range and learning the mechanics of shooting your pistol is not like a real gunfight.

Training and experimenting with paintball, simulated ammo, even rubber band guns you learn many things, the type of enlightenment one gets from the exchange of gunfire, and it can happen in the first second of training! Easy to read on paper, different to feel and learn. The single most, powerful, deadly, over-looked mistake in gun training is the fact that in gunfights, bullets are EXCHANGED! You are being SHOT AT while you are shooting. Only under the pressure of return fire do people really discover just how quickly they are shot while shooting.

This type of reciprocity training can be expensive and rigorous and it truly rocks the gun training world foundation, a world restricted by regulation, insurance, expensive facilities and a severe lack of creativity. But you don't always find God at a church, and you don't always have to learn gunfight tactics at a gun range. You can have rigorous gunfight training inside the gym walls of your local YMCA, or outside your back door.

When you say the words rigorous and YMCA, you suddenly lose a very large population of shooters. Shooters want to shoot their guns. For many shooters, shooting is really all about the guns and their love for them. For real survival combat instructors, guns are not a priority and are only one means to an end, truly a *tool.*

To see this, what if you advertised, "For today's 8 hour block at the range, we are going to wrestle with each other on the ground, and when you hear the whistle, you will pull and shoot your paintball gun into your training partner before he pulls his and shoots his into you. You can and should try to take his gun away from him if you can."

Sounds like great training! A real stress quick draw! Happens all the time on the mean streets. But, how many people are really up for that? How many will report to the paintball range and suit up for a rigorous day dodging bullets? Look at the attendees at your common shooting range. Many civilians show up as if they are about to play golf. Or many dress in a military shirt and pants, but have the heart of a golfer. Many enforcement officers must shoot in their uniforms and suits and return right back to work. How many officers or citizens can and will volunteer to spend a day rolling on the ground and practicing high stress, combat quick draws? Or low crawl between buildings to get a shot in on a paint baller? How many? Yet, so much real world combat occurs in this manner.

Entirely too much civilian, police and security shooting training is spent on shooting. Not nearly enough is spent on tactics, strategy, maneuvers, positioning, set-ups and dirty tricks. Conversely, too much military practice is spent searching and maneuvering and not enough time is spent shooting the various weapons and ordinance issued. The science of gun fighting is more about tricky, sneaky savvy than shooting paper targets using two-handed grips. General George S. Patton, one of the most remarkable men to serve in the United States military, said decades ago:

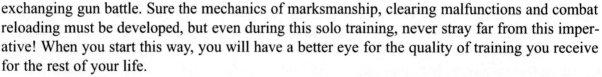

"It takes a certain mindset and ability to gun fight. Training this mental edge is severely lacking at the time and expense of standing around a public shooting range and wasting ammunition in the name of shooting courses."

I am committed, and therefore this CQCG course is committed, to the principle that from Day One of gun training, the practitioner must be mentally and physically introduced to the idea and feeling that he or she must perform in a bullet exchanging gun battle. Sure the mechanics of marksmanship, clearing malfunctions and combat reloading must be developed, but even during this solo training, never stray far from this imperative! When you start this way, you will have a better eye for the quality of training you receive for the rest of your life.

Learning to work your gun is but a layer of a gunfight. Being shot at while doing it is another layer of the million layers in a gunfight. What about the other 999,998 layers? Being in that driver's seat of a gunfight is different.

This is the trigger.
 This is the bullet.
  This is the sight.
   Now get ready for the million layers of combat.

Here are some sweeping generalizations we can post on the million layers...

1) Combat Stress Quick Draws in standing, kneeling and ground positions

2) Counters to Quick Draws

3) Functionality in all weather conditions

4) Functionality in all lighting conditions

5) Ambidextrous single-hand and double hand shooting

6) Tactical and/or stress combat reloading

7) Close quarter enemy weapon grabs and deflections

8) Close quarter captures and disarms

9) Knowledge and skill in unarmed combatives

10) Foot race to cover or escape

11) Vehicle race to cover or escape

12) Traversing all kinds of indoor and outdoor, urban and rural environments

13) Will to fight on after being shot

14) Will to survive

15) Will to win

16) Will to kill

17) Tremendous tactical, spontaneous problem-solving and trickery skills

18) Etc........

Studies and Observations 2) Carry Conditions of Your Weapon

Many individuals must carry their firearms under certain restrictions which promote or hinder quick draws. In the continuum of readiness, there are double-action and single-action operations, round chambered and un-chambered carries, and safeties-on and safeties-off choices or mandates.

Quick draws of pistols and long guns come from primary, fast access, carry sites or off the body or from very near lunge and reach areas. Beltline and thigh carries and shoulder holster are the most popular ways to carry a potential pistol quick draw weapon. Secondary sites like ankle or boot holsters, or inside bulletproof vests require more time to dig out the weapon for production. Quick draws of long guns come mostly from what are called *shoulder-carry* positions with slings.

Part of your quick draw is getting your weapon ready to fire. Many carry their weapons in a shoot-ready condition-hammer back and bullet in chamber, with no safeties or one safety engaged. Some are ordered by their superiors or their conscience to carry their weaponry in less than ready modes such as empty chamber or even unloaded.

Pistol Chamber and Shoot

Despite common sense, many police, security and militaries mandate that their people carry their semi-automatic pistols in their holsters with an empty chamber. This means that a bullet must be chambered, or slid from the top of the magazine into the chamber in front of the gun's barrel. Here, upon the trigger pull, the firing device strikes and ignites the bullet. Many citizens also carry their weapons in this manner.

Revolvers are often carried on an empty chamber in their cylinder, but with the first squeeze of the trigger, the revolver's cylinder is rotated to produce the next live round in top position to fall under the firing pin and fire.

There are two common ways to solve this problem with an unchambered semi-auto for a quick draw, the old holster version and the slide pull and shoot version. These techniques are called different things in different countries.

I was taught these two quick draw techniques in the mountains of northern South Korea by military supervisors in a world where the old-fashioned cavalry style flap holsters were required issue. The flap holster is still issued in some regions and jurisdictions, and while it does offer some inclement weather and hostile environment protection to handguns, it severely hinders your quick draw.

Pistol Chambering 1) Holster Chambering Quick Draw (QD)

This practice works in certain durable, stiff holsters. Many newer holsters, like ones of softer nylons, are too soft to support this mechanical action.

Step 1: Open the flap (if applicable).
Step 2: Grab the weapon.
Step 3: Extract the weapon a bit more than half way, and turn the handle out.
Step 4: Jam the weapon down hard, pushing the top of the gun against your
body. This forces the slide back and then pumps the round into the chamber.
Step 5: Draw and fire.

Pistol Chambering 2) Draw and Hand Chamber Quick Draw

Another method is to pull the slide back as you quick draw and seat a round in the firing chamber as you go to target. This can work if your other hand is not needed to fight off a close quarter combatant. In this series, the gun is vertical and the fingers cup the slide and pull it back.

Some systems hold the pistol turned into a horizontal position and work the slide back with thumb and fingers. With some weapons, should you depress the trigger during this process, when you let loose of the slide and it rams home, the trigger will be free and the pistol will fire. This can be discovered with an experimental dry-fire on a semi-auto by semi-auto basis.

This chambering takes precious time in the stress of combat and the no-chamber rules of security, military and police policies should be abolished. When you go into the arena, what exactly is the carry condition of your weapon? Is it ready to go? What will it take?

Studies and Observations 3) From Race Gun to Combat Gun, Carry Sites and the Holster Continuum

The artist and the fighter. Quick draws come from primary, fast access, carry sites or off the body from very near lunge and reach areas. Beltline and thigh carries and shoulder holsters are the most popular ways to carry a potential quick draw weapon. Secondary sites like ankle or boot holsters, or inside bulletproof vests require more time to dig out the weapon for production.

We have all seen carnival and circus pistol, quick draw artists and these high-speed shooting competitions. These people have special holsters and rigs that accelerate pre-planned performances. This is not the everyday gear of citizen, soldier and enforcement personnel. These quick draw rigs have little to zero weapon retention qualities. Competition rigs are usually bare slips of leather.

Retention holsters are engineered to prevent the enemy from stealing your pistol. This is done by limiting the angle of the quick draw to that of the carrier, and/or by installing release mechanisms on the holster not easily known to the enemy. Deviations from this angle can prevent quick draws. Law enforcement trainers note they have observed officers at the practice range having difficulty drawing their weapons from various retention holsters. This is a training issue that may be overcome in most cases: however, some retention holsters hinder chaotic positional quick draws such as in some ground fighting scenarios. The more safe and complex the holster, the less speed in the quick draw in less than perfect shooting stances. You must experiment with your quick draw from various standing, seated, kneeling and ground positions.

Carry Site Continuum

    1) Primary carry sites for *quick draws*

    2) Secondary carry sites for *back up*

    3) Tertiary carry sites for *lunge and reach* weapon grabs

Holster Continuum

    1) No holster (Instead, the weapon is inserted in the beltline or a pocket.)

    2) Retention holster with differing threat levels

    3) Normal holster with or without typical thumb break or strap

    4) Race gun competition holster

Studies and Observations 4) To Draw or Not to Draw

Many times the quick presentation of a pistol can scare off, bluff or freeze the enemy. Sometimes this bluff may not work. At times like this, another survival skill is re-holstering your weapon under stress because you cannot morally, ethically or legally use the piece on an unarmed man for example, and then must fight with two free hands. All weapons are drawn for two primary reasons:

> QD Reason 1: Weapon Presentation: To prevent violent action before it starts
> QD Reason 2: Weapon Firing: To stop violent action after it has begun

There is another vital issue in this "to draw or not to draw" question. Can you? Do you really have the time to draw and stop an incoming attacker with a stick, knife or other weapon? Pistols are notorious for not stopping people dead in their tracks. There are old commando parables about shooting men in the pelvis and dropping them, or delivering even head shots. But torsos and heads will bob while rushing you, making precise eyeball shoots difficult and the records and histories show these strategies often do not work. Do not believe that handgun rounds will always stop a rushing armed or unarmed attacker. You will need unarmed combative skills to support your firearm in close quarter combat.

Bullets and moving people make for strange and bewildering combinations. A nick on the scalp can send one football linebacker into a tailspin one time. Yet, a jackhammer hit on another's forehead may not stop an attacker as he takes eight more steps and stabs you.

A United States Federal Bureau of Investigation study discovered that in 98 percent of officer shootings, the armed offender shot first! *They scored a 90 percent hit ratio.* Usually, we – the good guys – respond to violence and the physical factors concerning reaction time come into play. This leaves us at a deficit. Police testing shows that if a person perceives a threat, such as the movement or quick draw of a weapon in the hands of another, it could take from .5 to 1.5 seconds for his or her brain to process that information and complete a reaction like going for his weapon. Even if your gun was already out predicting a perceived threat, in a half-ready posture, the average officer needs .73 seconds to raise the weapon up to the shooter's eye level to fire. Drawing from a holstered side arm will take much longer, with tests that show from 1.9 seconds or more may pass, depending upon the holster. Sometimes the only option you have is to react with your empty hands in extreme close quarters. Learn the unarmed combatives portion of the CQC Group, and pull that pistol when you think it's the right time.

Here, the cover arm takes the first shot. Was pulling your gun at this point the most appropriate action? Or was unarmed combatives the best option?

Studies and Observations 5) Pistol Gunfight Rules of 3
Many experts and studies have crunched the pistol combat numbers and have universally accepted these rules.

  – Many to most pistol gunfights last about 3 seconds.

  – Many to most pistol gunfire exchanges involve more than 3 rounds.

  – Many gunfighters exchange rounds within 3 yards.

Worldwide studies have shown that 95 percent of enforcement shootings occur at 21 feet or less. Seventy-five percent occur at nine feet or less. This CQCG course is designed around these conditions, starting its training progression in a range where most pistol gunfights occur – within approximately 3 to 4 yards and with a skill where so many pistol and long gun gunfights start – a desperate quick draw. Extreme close quarters starts from a zero sternum-to-sternum base line, to some three yards away from you in any direction. Here, the enemy is within a lunge and reach from grabbing you or your pistol with both his hands or with his free hand. Or, he is a short jump, lunge and reach from you. Your study and practice should reflect these circumstances and work accordingly.

Studies and Observations 6) Pistol Quick Draw Basic Steps
Smooth first. Speed later. The following four steps are universally accepted. The fifth I have added because it is part of the combat quick draw process and vital to survival.

  QD Basic Step 1 – Grab the pistol the same way with the same grip.

  QD Basic Step 2 – Straight forearm in line with the barrel.

  QD Basic Step 3 – Disengage any safeties, and/or perform any tasks unique to your
          holster and weapon, such as chambering a round.

  QD Basic Step 4 – Perform a clean trigger pull that does not pull your barrel off of
          the enemy.

  QD Basic Step 5 – deliver and duck, move to cover or concealment to minimize your
          visible profile – the outline your enemy sees. Cover stops bullets. Concealment hides
          you but does not stop bullets. Every gunfight is intrinsically linked with your surroundings. Military, police and citizen shooting studies prove that over 90 percent of shooters able to reach cover survived the shooting. Shoot and move. Move and shoot. This will be covered extensively in *CQCG Training Mission Six.*

A slight change from your practiced quick draw pattern may interfere with your under-stress, developed reflex. Clothing can interfere. Holster changes can interfere. Weapon changes can certainly interfere.

Studies and Observations 7) The Empty or Other Hand

In a perfect world, we shoot with our gun clamped into a shooter's vise on a solid table. But the world isn't perfect. The other end of that continuum is firing one-handed, weak-side – because our strong side is wounded – while on a dead run, in the mud, in the dark, in a rainstorm. Make that a blizzard.

I want you to shoot with two hands all the time. It steadies you on target and reduces recoil. But we can't always do this. Even in longer ranges, we can't always shoot with two hands. Our hand can be called upon to perform a whole host of tasks, like hauling prisoners and wounded comrades, climbing, moving and pushing furniture and bystanders, lugging gear, distracting, throwing something, striking, blocking, pushing, deflecting, grabbing, etc.

The muscle memory of mindless, mandatory two-hand grip shooting can be simplistic, dangerous training. You may have to start shooting while shoving the enemy away, or pushing over a table while shooting and a host of other tasks. Become mindful, not mindless.

There is but a micro-second between grabbing the pistol in your holster and acquiring a healthy, two hand-ed, stable grip, it is just that statistically the enemy is too close for you to do it.

The Shooting Support Hand Continuum

If you can go to two hands, a second firm hand can help in a continuum of support. On one end is the strict top-on-bottom resting platform, the other, the isometric push/pull grip. I demonstrate both here because often one's perfect grip on a pistol will lie somewhere in between and will vary by two factors, the size of one's hand and the size of one's gun.

Beware The Panic Hand Quick Draw

Will the *other* hand do the right thing? Even veteran operators, under attack stress, can forget and try to pull their weapon with two hands, one hand on the gun handle, the other hand stretched across the body and grasping for the holster as if this steadies the holster for a better quick draw. I have seen this in actual police work and in schools that I have attended and conducted. The person stands tall and delivers fire on the firing line, but when charged by a brute, or receiving incoming rounds, these same people lose that *firing line cool* and fumble in this two-handed quick draw manner.

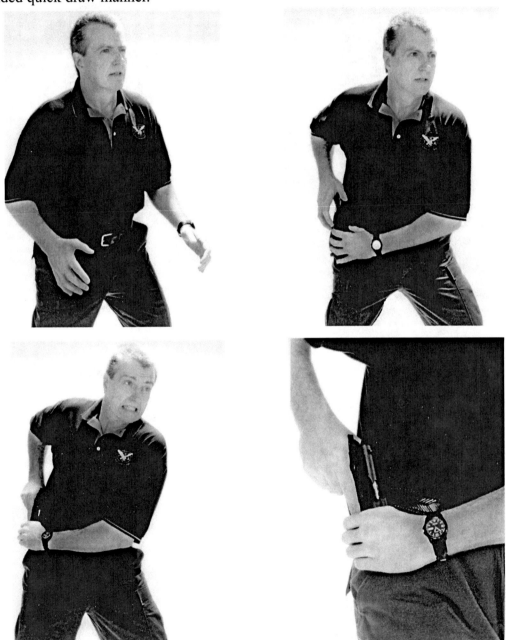

This panic, second hand assist on the holster may prevent you from using that free hand to counter a close quarter enemy. Some experts say the unnecessary, untrained movement actually slows down your quick draw.

The Empty Hand Clears Clothing

Here is a plainclothes method I was taught by federal agents back in the 1980's that used the opposite hand to clear a jacket. You grab the side of a sport/suit coat or jacket and pull. This twists the garment on your body, hopefully granting easier access to your weapon.

You'll still need your gun hand to help clear a path to your weapon. This may change with differing outerwear. Experiment with the clothing you have.

The Empty Hand Protects the Body

The hand should be used to protect the body in some way, not thrown up and out to the side, as shown in the photo on the left, which serves no purpose at all. This hand up and out is often mindlessly replicated by classic point-shooters.

The flight paths of bullets can be influenced by the bones and mass of the hand or arm.

Studies and Observations 7) Quick Draw Overview

You will have to quick draw in the following predicaments in bright and low light (most civilian/police/security gunfights occur between 6 p.m. and 6 a.m. in low light or no light conditions.)

Standing QDs	Kneeling QDs	Ground QDs
QDs to the front	QDs to the sides	QDs behind you
QDs above you	QDs below you	QDs on the move
QDs from vehicles		

Studies and Observations 8) Quick Draw Positions

When you pull your pistol, you are limited to using a one or a two-handed grip and in only a few quick fire positions. Both grips act in combination with the positions.

The following are samples of the basics. I am not advocating any one of them in particular. I want you to know all of them and practice all of them hundreds of times. There is no football scoring stance, no home run hitting stance. There is no one gun fighting stance. Combat is balance in motion. Stationary stances are really more training methods and issues than a combat tactic. Transition, transition, transition. The combat quick draw equation is drawing, shooting and moving almost at the same time.

Remember, no matter what you want your end grip to be, all quick draws begin with one hand.

The Standing Triangle Shooting Stances

The basic triangle shooting stances are called many different titles around the world. Range shooters often stand erect and proudly while shooting, yet in combat, the reflex in our body's sympathetic nervous system causes us to crouch down. The triangle also puts our arm bones across our chest giving us some level of cover. The standing triangle stances are:

QD High Triangle) Arms extended and body very frontal.

QD Bladed High Triangle)
Arms somewhat extended and body bladed from the enemy.

QD Low Triangle) Arms tucked in or somewhat extended and body very frontal.

QD Bladed Low Triangle) Arms tucked in and body bladed from the enemy.

The Standing Single-Hand Stances

One Hand High) *This gets the weapon up into the famous "flash sight" position in front of your nose.*

One Hand Low) *Weapon keep on the side for extreme CQC. Statistics tell us to practice this most of the time.*

One Hand Center-Line) *Weapon brought under the nose line or center line of your body for natural shooting instinct.*

One Hand "Dueler") *A slim target profile.*

Some notes on the Dueler. To the dismay of many modern range-based instructors, the Dueler who turns sideways and becomes a skinny, slinky target, dodging the enemy's barrel while shooting and moving to cover, is shot less and survive more simulated ammo training sessions than the two-hand shooters who stand still, shoot and deliver in triangle stances.

One Hand to the Rear) *Turn and shoot the enemy behind you. This first single-handed shot is quicker than waiting for your body to catch up to form into a two-handed grip.*

Keep shooting as you turn. Get the two-handed grip if you can. Get moving!

Knee-High Shooting Stances

Many shooters instinctively drop really low depending upon the nature and distance of the threat. This is appropriate in some situations. However, it does limit your mobility to run for cover. It is worthy of practice for times when the drop and shoot is smart. You do not have to support your arms atop your knee or thigh.

One Knee Supported.

Quick draw. Down on one knee. How do you best support your shooting hand? If possible with your other hand. If you can't, then there are three ways, on the side of the knee area, on the knee, or the thigh.

But remember, you can shoot this low without the knee at all. Simply use a two-hand grip that you might use when standing.

Two-hand shooting. One knee stance.

Leg side support. One knee stance.

Elbow to knee support. One knee.

Elbow (and forearm) to thigh support. One knee.

I was instructed decades ago by both military and police experts to avoid what is called the *joint-on-joint* roll. That is in this case, elbow-bone atop knee-bone. The premise is that this connection will rock and not offer a stable platform to shoot from. Instructors advised us to place our elbow and/or forearm atop our thigh. In the 1990's, several very elite special team members told me their current doctrine was to avoid the elbow positioned atop a *mushy* thigh and that bone-to-bone was solid and was preferable. I'll let you decide from your experience.

Two Knee Position Shooting

Two-fisted triangle grip with two knees down.

Many times desperate combatants under fire have been photographed, filmed or confessed to dropping and quickly shooting in this manner. It hinders follow-up mobility, but it seems to happen reflexively at times of explosion and as shock waves of a firefight ripple through the air.

The above photo displays a frontal triangle. Of course your body could be bladed.

Ground Shooting Positions

Many shooters instinctively drop on their back depending upon the nature and distance of the threat. This is wholly appropriate in some situations; however, it does limit your mobility to move for cover. It is worthy of practice for times when the drop back and shoot is smart. Also, try to imagine this draw while being shoved back off your feet.

You round off your body and roll back. Try to keep an eye on your enemy. This also helps you from banging your head on the ground. Do not shoot your knees or feet, but fire as quickly as possible. Legs spread, you are a broad target for direct fire or for rounds skipping off the ground. Hook your feet and make yourself as small a target as humanly possible to your enemy. Try to keep those toes out of the way!

Beware the Sideways Ground Shooting Position

This is when a shooter drops almost sideways to an enemy (shown to the left), a classic leftover known mostly from World War II era combatives. Sadly, this is still being taught in many schools. By doing this, the shooter makes himself a full body target for both direct and indirect fire. Whenever possible, you should make yourself as small a target as possible.

Rounds can hit your whole body directly or by skipping off the ground.

Make yourself as small a target as possible.

Weary after hours of lying prone shooting pistols on a Army range, I tried this hand configuration. The pistol came up to eye level and secured a steady sight picture. It worked well for my aching neck and tired arms.

Many ranges are smartly asking their practitioners to drop back and practice shooting over their heads like this. Often they add a roll, then shoot, then roll.

Studies and Observations 9) Quick Draw from Automobiles

Law enforcement and security patrols have long struggled with the dilemma of quick drawing, as well as quickly escaping from automobiles. To make matters worse, mandatory seat belt laws have confounded the process. Seat belts really impede quick exits and quick draws. Angry citizens, who have been receiving *no seat belt* tickets for years now, often complain when they see officials without belts engaged. Here are two methods I have tested that might help you. I hope you will experiment with them in your specific vehicles, and with your guns, autos and holsters.

Here the seat belt is run under the holster, giving a clean access path to the weapon.

Here, the seat belt is run under a leg. This also gives the viewing public the appearance of an engaged seat belt.

Studies and Observations 10) The Bluffing Barney and the Two Jacks
In our study progression we have developed the quick draw. At this point our gun is out either for a presentation to prevent violence before it starts, or to shoot to stop violence while it is happening. We will start with the subject of presentation.

I fear a society where enforcement and military are timid about pulling their guns from their holsters. When the time comes, they need to pull, and they hesitate. Don't believe for an instant this politically correct and dangerous dictum:

"If you need to pull your gun, then you need to pull it and shoot it. If you didn't need to shoot instantly, then you aren't justified in pulling out the pistol in the first place."

These are the shallow, naive, ignorant and/or stupid words of a rear-echelon desk-rider who has not only never seen the *elephant,* he has also never even seen a titmouse. There are just some times that the barrel of a gun, a mean face and an ugly growl gets the job done.

"The mightiest warrior never has to use his sword," is an old martial arts expression. This plays to the reputation of a person. Combine that with a solid command presence and you lesson the chance of having to fight. Many researchers say that the average message is 90 percent non-verbal and 10 percent verbal. Constructing the body and language message is crucial to survival. Consider my litany of *Barney and the Two Jacks.*

If you must quick draw to shut down possible violence or interrupt violence, your bluff must be effective, and you must have a command presence. If Mayberry PD's Barney Fife draws down on a killer, his shaking voice and hand will convince the suspect he has a chance that Barney will not use his weapon and could be overcome. If Jack Webb draws down on a killer, his dedication to rules is a tip-off to the killer that Webb can be pushed and toyed with for a chance to escape, especially if the killer is unarmed. There is little chance Jack Webb will make good his threat to shoot an unarmed man. If Jack Nicholson draws down on a killer, in fine "Here's Johnny!" fashion, the killer realizes that this Jack is crazed and is liable to twist off and kill him for little to no reason. Which method of acting would you use to bluff? You do not have to assume the complete Jack Nicholson persona, but find one and practice it.

There is a gun fighting school of thought that states you should not threaten the enemy with something that you cannot actually do. But this destroys the trick, bluff, the Jack Nicholson threat, and that threat has frozen many in their tracks and has worked hundreds of thousands of times in civilian, military and enforcement situations. If the bluff doesn't work? At least you tried! Take a deep breath, re-holster up and go do what you have to do next.

Studies and Observations 11) Point vs. Aim?

In a few words, point shooting is shooting based on hand/eye coordination instinct, without finding the sights of your gun to aim and shoot. Aim shooting is using the aligned sights of your firearm. Here they are listed in connection with vision.

Binocular Vision (instinctive point shooting)

Point shooting is best performed with both eyes open and over your gun. Often you must shoot from near your hip because the opponent is way too close. It seems that looking at your target, specifically where you want your bullet to land, steers your body to instinctively shoot near where you wish your bullet to land. Many combat vets like the advantage of seeing all of the battlefield with two eyes open.

Telescope (Monocular) Vision (aim with gun sights shooting)

In order to best access your gun sights, close one of your eyes and seek to align the rear and front sights of your weapon.

There are two training groups in a constant feud over these two topics. Those who promote aim-shooting are eager to report any dismal training and real life miss ratios of point shooters. Their quoted police shooting studies never tout distance to technique, opting simply to brag on their agenda that "agencies who teach point shooting do poorly." NEVER are these studies discussed in direct reference to the distances between target and shooters. Who really knows the distance ratios figured into their case study stats? Possibly, incidents where officers are at a dead run shooting at a moving hijacked bus? However, at the end of the aim-shoot-only speech, is always the whispered caveat, "Oh, by the way-you can't use your sights if the enemy is real close." Well, that happens to be more than half, if not most, of the time.

If 100 point-shooting people shot a target 5 feet away, the results would almost always be good to excellent. If this same 100 point-shooting people shot at a target at 50 feet? Not good. Clear-headed people simply see that when the enemy is too close and there is no time to aim, you must point and shoot. When there is time and space, you should aim. It is the purpose of *Training Mission One* to study the pistol quick draw in conjunction with very close quarter combat. We concern ourselves with pistol shooting up to about 20 feet, but within 9 yards is really emphasized.

Facing the hard facts. In the majority of real world shooting incidents, where are the classic stances, the sight alignments, Zen breathing, etc.? They were done in a perfect training world to provide a foundational understanding of pure marksmanship and gun machine mechanics. You must then free yourself from all this structure to succeed in the unpredictable chaos of combat.

Studies and Observations 12) The Big Exchange

While you are trying to point or aim shoot, the enemy is trying to do the same to you.

Two or more shooting at you.

Some 40 percent of police shootings involve two or more opponents. Almost all military shootings involve two or more (sometimes hundreds in your influential line of fire). There are no stats on civilian/criminal encounters. This is a great motivation to possess larger capacity magazines.

Criminals do well shooting at you.

As mentioned before, FBI studies show that in 98 percent of the incidents where officer were involved in shootings, the criminals had a 90 percent hit ratio. The officers had a 41 percent ratio. It is believed that officers are usually firing back and second. Eighty percent of the criminals interviewed report little to zero shooting training and rely on instinct shooting.

Soldiers do well shooting at you.

Improved shooting methods and increased semi-auto and automatic fire have increased the firing rates and skills of most militaries of the world.

Synergy Quick Draw Drills

Pistol QD Drill 1) The Two Hand Space Awareness Drill

Two training partners stand facing each other, one arm's length apart. The trainee has a training weapon in his or her holster. The trainer is unarmed. The purpose of the drill is to teach physical distance awareness as it relates to a draw into a two-handed grip. The trainer plans to interrupt the trainee's quick draw. How far away can an enemy be before the trainee can successful-

ly draw the pistol into a standard two-hand grip? Start increasing the distance with experimentation. This is nothing but a space awareness drill. After a series of experiments, the trainee will finally have a realistic, working knowledge of when a two-handed grip might be safely achieved when standing before an aggressor.

The distance an opponent can cover in front of you when they lunge and grab is often deceiving. This teaches a student this spatial awareness.

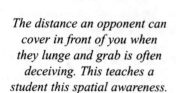

Pistol QD Drill 2) Space, Stress and Speed Awareness Drills. Two training partners stand before each other, both armed with weapons loaded with simulated ammunition with holsters and gear as every day, realistic as possible. They go palm-to-palm. Draw and shoot.

Just a space, stress and speed awareness drill.

They see who can draw and shoot first, but this study goes deeper. Who-shoots-who first is only a part. How many times they shoot each other is more likely the evaluation. I have conducted numerous training sessions with a vast variety of groups from complete novices to shooting experts and instructors. Both die frequently and equally, with the exception of the novices who are free enough in mind and body to turn sideways and start shooting and jumping away and are therefore wounded less. The ones wounded more? The two-hand shooters who just stand there as though they were on a shooting range seem to be shot more. These encounters reveal more of the ugly truth about gun fighting. How easily and quickly we are shot!

     Round 1: Both armed and quick draw.
     Round 2: One armed and one unarmed. Unarmed tries to disrupt the QD.
     Round 3: Both armed again – this time, wiser.

By Round 3, the practitioners learn trying to quick draw all the time causes them to be shot while shooting back. A no-win situation. Fresh from Round 2, where they charged in and countered the pistol quick draw, in Round 3 they must make a choice to draw or charge in to counter. This is a fantastic drill to gauge space, speed, options and response.

     I have maintained a journal of events as I have watched many students practice these drills. I have seen pistols fly through the air – lost in the stress of the confrontation, retention holsters prevent quick draws, inside-the-pants holsters that come right out with the pistol. Many of these acts were by range trained pistoleros/experts who have never stared down such face-off stress. Just a simple pair of rubber band guns can bring out much enlightenment.

Pistol QD Drill 3) Ground Quick Draws

The trainer punches or shoves the trainee to the ground. The trainer is standing. The trainee grounded. The trainer circles the downed trainee. The trainee spins to keep in a position to observe his attacker. At some point, one of the two goes for his gun. A simulated shooting occurs.

Drawing a pistol horizontally is quite different than vertically, especially with certain retention holsters.

I ask that this drill begin with the trainee punched or pushed down so that the trainee may experience this and learn to recover from it. The trainer should spend a few seconds circling the trainee so the downed person may learn to maneuver on the ground.

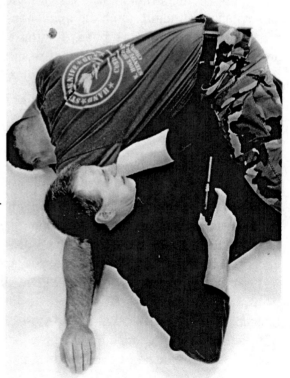

Pistol QD Drill 4) The Ground Roll Pistol Quick Draw Drill

Here we are again using the ground roll format. Start in any ground position and assign the trainee the task of a pistol quick draw and shoot when possible. Remember not to jam the barrel into the enemy as it might prevent the mechanical function of the semi-auto (more on this later).

An unforgettable practice, great awareness, experience and endurance building practice.

Pistol QD Drill 5) Block, Pass and Pin Quick Draw Drill

A practitioner can develop extreme close quarter, one-handed quick draws in many ways, but the following is a two-person drill inspired by martial art systems. This block, pass and pin synergy drill takes the exact same six steps, or beats, between two partners that was previously introduced in the unarmed combatives portion of this book. Partners first master the six steps/beats and then execute half-beat inserts. In this case, we use pistol quick draws when possible. After reviewing the six steps, or beats, here is how you quick draw on beat 3 1/2.

Step/Beat 1: Left hand blocks an attack.

Step/Beat 2: Right hand passes the attack.

Step/Beat 3: Left hand pins the attack.

Step/Beat 3 1/2: He pushes and pulls.

You must practice this format further by:

Variation 1: Draw on other half-beats.

Variation 2: Draw from cross draw carries.

Variation 3: The opponent really charges back at you to interfere with your draw after you have shoved him.

Variation 4: Perform the drill starting with the gun drawn, finger off the trigger. Many armed personnel start a conflict with a drawn weapon, realize they cannot shoot the opponent and then must fight. Re-holstering under stress is an important survival skill. Practice re-holstering on some half beats.

Take care not to shoot your hip or leg in the stress of re-holstering. It has happened. One trick is to slap the side of your pistol vertical against the holster, slide the handgun up, over and into the holster, thereby going by feel alone. Snap it in place if you can for retention purposes.

The block. Beat/Step 1

The pass. Beat 2. Take care with that gun!

Re-holster and...

The pin. Beat 3. 3 1/2 shove hard for space.

...hands free fighting.

Variation 5: Perform the drill on your back. Remember many high threat retention holsters will not allow a quick draw in many ground positions.

Variation 6: Continue to experiment and invent new variables.

This is a great drill to develop CQC pistol quick draw and battle. It simulates very close, forearm-to-forearm conflict and gives a practitioner familiarity with this common combat crash and clash. Each variation is like a testing ground to give you experience in what you like and don't like and what you think you can get away with. Remember, you have to decide if you should, or even can, quick draw the weapon. Often you must simply fight with your empty hands. If you do pull the weapon and the opponent is unarmed, you may try a command presence order or bluff.

Pistol QD Drill 6) Walking and Running Quick Draws

The trainee starts from a distance. He approaches the trainer at a walking pace or a running pace. The trainer draws and the trainee must respond with a draw and fire while in motion.

Walk or run toward a trainee. The trainer will give you a cue to draw. The best cue is drawing a weapon. While moving, draw and if simulated ammo and gear is available, fire at the trainer.

Extensive "run, shoot, cover" strategies and tactics will be presented in *CQCG Training Mission Six.*

You must learn to quick draw while in motion.

Once the shooting starts, the trainee can decide to drop and shoot, go for cover or whatever he or she sees fit to do under the circumstances. Enough cannot be emphasized about running. Warriors run. They train to run. They cover the ground of urban and rural terrain. They know how to run in, under, up and around things, thus the emphasis on obstacle courses for military and smart police training. There is a *speed run,* that is very upright like a track star crossing the ribbon-breaking finish line. Then there is the *combat run,* tucked over, ducking rounds, powerful like a football linebacker coming in for freight train collision. Learn to do both.

Pistol QD Drill 7) Dropping Quick Draws

The trainee starts from a distance. He approaches the trainer at a walking pace or a running pace. The trainer draws, and the trainee must respond with a draw, drop and fire while in motion. It is good to run the drill around potential cover objects. The shooter should get to cover as quickly as possible and shoot while doing so.

Variation 1)
Here the author drops to a one knee barricade style position at Gun Town USA, where he once regularly taught gun combatives.

Variation 2)
The shooter drops to the ground.

Pistol QD Drill 8) The Slap Leather Drill

Want to increase your quick draw speed dramatically? Get your hand to your gun faster! It requires no mechanical skill such as the tasks involved for your hand AFTER it gets to the gun handle, like unsnapping thumb breaks, twisting for retention holsters, undoing safeties, etc. Watch any group at the range try to shoot for time. The whistle blows and invariably almost all of them do not access their pistol very quickly, or as quickly as you know they could. Imagine their hands were on a hot stove and they jerked it back from the hot flame or got an electric shock.

Even when you order them to do it faster, they have no real idea how slow they are, how fast they could be, or how to get "stove-touching" hot. Start by standing behind your student and put your palm on his holster. Let him get ready, much like on a firing line or street gun fight position and play the *slap leather game*. Tap his holster lightly as you yank your hand back and challenge him to try and catch your hand. Let him catch your hand the first few times.

Then get faster. He will get faster. He now has a physical experience, the feel of speed, to relate to. Make him remember the feeling of this hand speed.

Something in the Gun Hand Already? The Drop and Draw!

There was old advice in policing that one must always keep their gun hand empty to enable a quick draw. This was particularly stressed when police officers conduct a traffic stop. You were warned never to hold your clipboard or flashlight in your gun hand while approaching and interviewing the driver. But, advisors never mentioned what to do about the distracting and subsequent act of studying a driver's license, or writing a ticket that occupies the gun hand. You could be shot while your eyes and hands are busy writing the ticket.

If you are going to grab the handle of your pistol for a quick draw, you are going to open up your hand anyway. If anything is already in your hand, such as a clipboard or pen, in the act of opening your hand to acquire your handgun, you drop the board while grabbing the pistol. This *drop and draw* is smart range practice for any street operator.

Pistol Quick Draw Option Awareness Combat Scenarios

Pistol QD Combat Scenario 1) The Interview Stance Scenarios – Sample Studies

The suspicious person stands before you. He may be a real threat. Right now he is a potential threat. How you act, what you say and how you stand may incite him or de-escalate him. Should he flare into attack, you need to be ready both mentally and physically. In terms of physics, you need what we call in the police profession, an interview stance.

Every person needs an interview stance – that is a balanced relaxed position, body slightly bladed from a potential suspect or threat. Keep a safe distance for reaction time. Your arms should be ready. I have been teaching such a position in police academies since 1985, where my arms are slightly and lightly crossed. They are barely touching and not at all trappable. From the suspect's or observer's perspective, I am inoffensive, but in one instant I can push, block, punch and draw my gun. You may choose to fight empty-handed! However, this is a weapon quick draw drill.

In a series of variations, have a trainer stand in front of you. He suddenly strikes, pushes or makes a furtive move to a common weapon carry site like he is going to pull a weapon.

You can:
– block
– push
– strike
– and draw, if needed.

Command presence and the bluff take over. Can't shoot? Holster, spray and/or take hand-to-hand action.

Every combat scenario needs a finish, so you must make a choice of what comes next should you decide to pull your pistol. If he is unarmed, then you bluff for a surrender. If the bluff doesn't work, law enforcement usually then re-holsters and moves to the next plan of lesser force. Civilians and military personnel may still be able to shoot, depending upon the circumstances. Always ask yourself the question, "what comes next?"

Remember the *drop and draw drill* mentioned two pages earlier? Use the interview stance but have a trainee hold a clipboard, or papers or a flashlight. On cue from the opponent, drop it all and draw.

Pistol QD Combat Scenario 2)
Countering the Close Quarter Pistol Threat – A Sample Study
This actual problem has arisen many times in robberies, kidnappings and killings surprising armed citizens, police and military. The enemy has gotten the surprise, sudden and angry *drop* on you, his gun up to, or very near the neck. This is a common, impulsive intimidation tactic.

At the right second....

...clear the barrel from you. Grab the gun!

Draw and shoot as many times as needed to put the enemy down and out.

Clear the barrel. Grabbing the gun can render it to a no-shot or one-shot operation. Draw your gun and start shooting. All in a second. Work this scenario with weapons that shoot simulated ammunition. In the presence of bystanders, try to steer the enemy's pistol away from the innocent.

Pistol QD Combat Scenario 3) Pistol Counters Snap Shooter Rifle – A Sample Study

This actual problem has arisen many times in robberies, kidnappings and killings upon armed citizens, police and military. The enemy has gotten the surprise, sudden and angry *drop* on you, his long gun up to, or very near your torso. Suddenly, he decides to shoot and signals this intent with the typical *snapshooting* motion of raising the barrel. This is a do or die signal for you to act. This is a common, impulsive intimidation tactic.

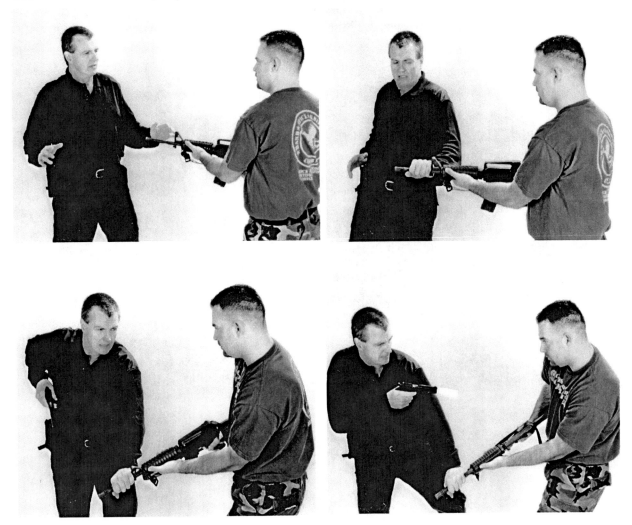

Clear the barrel by grabbing the gun. Draw and start shooting. All in a second. Shoot as needed until the enemy is down and out. Work this scenario with weapons that shoot simulated ammunition. In the presence of bystanders. Try to steer the enemy's barrel away from the innocent.

Some textbook worshipping instructors will comment on how this pistol must cross over your forearm in these scenarios. If you feel the need to shoot under your arm and can, then do so. But, these are ugly, dangerous situations. Clear your arm and fire center mass. When I practice this scenario with simulated ammo, I look at and point the pistol at the clavicle and fire multiple rounds. It is psychologically important for the trainee to see those rounds land on the enemy's chest.

Pistol QD Combat Scenario 4)
Pistol Counters Knife While Ground Fighting – A Sample Study
This is a worst case scenario. The enemy is atop you with a knife. View the following steps as general solutions that can apply to different situations. There are two major problems half way through the scenario. One problem is when the enemy lets go of your hand to prevent his head from hitting the ground. The second problem is when he hangs onto your arm. The first step is to push hard and upward. We hope this enlists the reflexive downward force then you reverse your push and pull his arms downward with his energy.

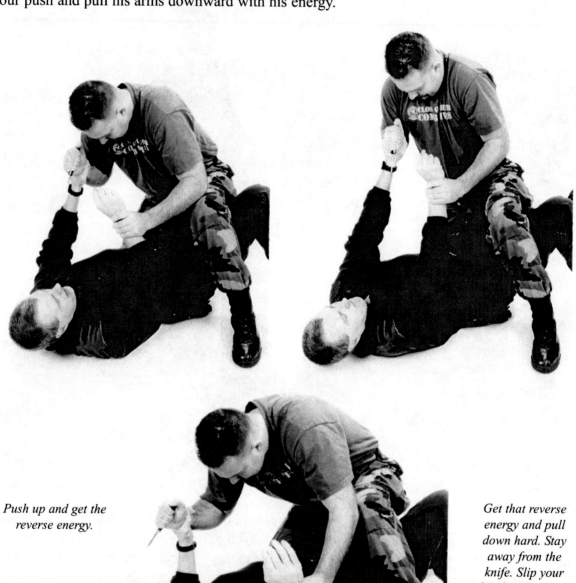

Push up and get the reverse energy.

Get that reverse energy and pull down hard. Stay away from the knife. Slip your head and neck to your right...

I have taught these steps many times, and to my surprise, the first time the attacker feels this fall, they let go of my right hand to *post,* or catch themselves as if their head will hit the ground. A knee strike to their rear helps this cause. This is the first problem, the easier one to solve, because he has let go of my gun hand. I am still trying to maintain a death grip on his weapon-bearing limb. I reach down, quick draw my pistol and since he is still holding a knife in his other hand, I fire until he is finished. I may need a knee to bash him and free up some body-to-body space to get at the pistol.

WARNING! Practice ground quick draws with your retention holster. You may have great difficulties.

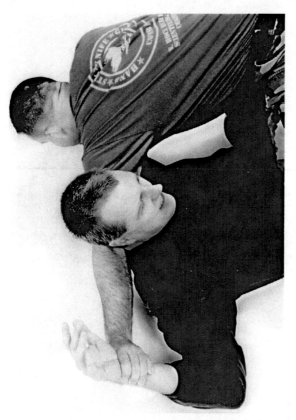

The second study problem occurs when the attacker does not let go of your right hand. Raise your right hand above your head. Scoop your head under his arm. You may need another knee strike to his rear to gain some space. Now, pull your arm down. Bridge your body and push against his arm to get a push, pull release of your gun hand.

Draw and fire as needed. Since he is still brandishing a knife. Prepare yourself for the close concussion of the pistol report. Work this scenario with weapons that shoot simulated ammunition.

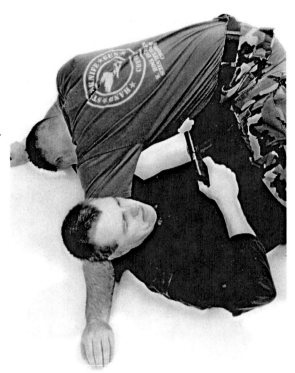

WARNING! It is not uncommon in the heat of such close quarters fighting for people to jam their pistols into the sides of the attacker. Many semi-automatics will not fire in this manner because with the slide pressed against someone and forced back, the weapon will be *out of battery*. I have seen many experts forget this in the stress of the ground struggle.

Pistol Quick Draw Summary

It is important to understand that you are not learning how to combat quick draws and/or gun-fights unless you are feeling the stress of someone drawing on you and shooting back at you. Unless you are under this type of reciprocal stress, you are just recreational/hobby shooting, or learning the machine mechanics of your gun as a precursor to start combat training. Simulated ammunition will create a revolution in combat firearms training.

The moves must first be learned in solo practice. The mechanics of the weapon must be learned. Then comes the return fire. The exchange of bullets. Simulated ammo training will cull the gun-lovers, and paper plunkers from the real gun combatives practitioners. The stress combat quick draw is the first real, giant step toward survival.

Many real-world opponents are shot from the unusual grips shown above and below.

Here they are again in real-life application. Practice these ugly firing positions much?

Long Gun Quick Draws: From Sling Carry to Combat

Ambush!

Ambushes and surprise attacks struck down the greatest armies of the world. Upon attack, the intended victims had to snap instantly into war mode from eating, walking, sitting around, talking, daydreaming or even sleeping. Even posted guards or patrols function in varying degrees of readiness and respond depending upon the circumstances.

Once alerted, they must raise their weapons to fire. Sometimes these weapons are locked away such as in Pearl Harbor, or nearby, or slung around a shoulder. Even animal hunters often snatch their weapons up when surprise game appears. This is not a SWAT problem, as they arrive prepped, up and ready, and the subject matter falls off their training radar.

In 2001, I was teaching a U.S. military group and I asked them if they were versed in shoulder carry rifle quick draws. To a man, this large ground force, armed with M-4s with single strap slings and bound for the Middle East, had never been taught a single one. This prompted me to record a base of study on the subject, so as to keep the techniques alive and available.

Main Uses of the Sling

In this segment we explore long gun quick draws, sometimes called *dismounts,* from various shoulder and sling carries. One might assume this information is taught at common military basic training, police academies or hunter safety classes. It is not. In fact, ask a common citizen, soldier or enforcement troop to suddenly pull their slung weapon into a shooting position and they will grab the strap on their chest and yank the long gun off their shoulder, sending it into orbit around their body, left only to be snatched in the air on the first pass if possible. Then the person must manipulate the weapon into a firing position.

There are two general types of long gun quick draws. One is a lunge and reach, where the weapon is nearby and you must get to it. The second quick draw is right off your body from its carry position, usually from a sling or in some cases clipped to or strung to a tactical vest. Elite military and special police tactical units often use clip and lanyard devices. This study will cover the most common single strap shoulder-sling quick draws. The main uses of a sling are:

Stand down. The sling offers relaxation.

The sling frees hands for combat, climbing or other tasks.

Sling Use 1) Stand-Down Carries. The sling offers a way to carry the weapon on your person in non-shooting situations from simply waiting in a coffee line to hand-to-hand combat. Further methods and variations of these non-shooting sling carries will be listed later in this essay.

Sling Use 2) General Shooting Support. The sling helps you with overall balance and secures the weapon during presentation and combat.

Sling Use 3) Tango Shooting Support. Wrapping the sling around your lead arm offers more barrel control for precision shooting. Note the sling wrapped around the lead arm.

Sling Use 4) Crawling. An infantryman learns to love the ground. Weapons can be carried during low crawls in various positions. The sling offers a variety of options. But tactics can call for crawling and other combat maneuvers that mandate the sling be secured, or wrapped around the weapon in some manner so as not to catch or hook nearby items as you travel.

Sling Use 5) Miscellaneous. In the field, there are some miscellaneous uses for slings, from makeshift clotheslines to tourniquets for the severely wounded.

The Basic Quick Draws from Sling Carries

Maximize your combat quick draw by taking note of the beginning carry positions in each of the following photo series. Reckless and unplanned carries will not allow you a quick draw and add multiple, unnecessary steps that could cost you your life in combat.

The consummate gunfighter can shoot well from both right and left-handed positions. Work toward that goal, but most people cannot train this extensively. A strong-side carry is when the weapon is hanging by your strong and coordinated hand. Right-handed people usually pull the trigger with their right trigger finger, vice-versa for lefties. A weak-side carry is when the weapon is hanging on the weak side and a quick draw must deliver the trigger to the strong-side trigger finger.

The quick draw firing positions will be from the hip to the shoulder. Under gunfire, the human sympathetic nervous system usually causes a person to crouch, a movement very conducive to raising the weapon up simultaneously to fire. The weapon can be carried on your body in these following combinations. Equipment and gear carried along with mission specifics will cause the variances. Here is a list of the main variables:

1) Strong side – weapon hanging down on your strong side.

2) Weak side – weapon hanging down on your weak side. Sometimes elite troops with pistols on their strong side will opt to carry their long weapon on their weak side.

3) Front hang – across the chest, the butt of the weapon should point to the strong side for quick access.

4) Rear hang – cross the back, the barrel of the weapon downward and may point to the strong side or weak side. A proper quick draw can produce a good firing position.

5) Barrel up.

6) Barrel down.

7) Sling wrapped on the same shoulder as weapon.

8) Cross sling – sling wrapped on opposite shoulder of weapon and over your head.

9) Head loop. The sling is looped around the neck, and the weapon is hanging some where on the chest.

The G.I. Quick Draw
This is the most common carry, barrel up with the sling and weapon on the same strong side.

The weak hand grabs the weapon and lifts, helping the sling clear any load-bearing gear and/or shoulder epaulets.

The strong hand slips through the weapon and sling as the body blades away from the enemy.

The hands manipulate into shooting position.

The fighter engages gunfire with the enemy.

The Commando Quick Draw

This is when the fighter has the sling strung over his head and the weapon hangs horizontal under his or her *strong side* arm. This is the extreme readiness position. All the troop has to do is grab the weapon properly and fire from the hip or raise up for better target acquisition. This quick grab and fire also holds true for the weapon that is looped around the neck and hanging up front. Every weapon has differing attachments for slings. Often the weapon hung in this manner, allowed to hang free, will hang sideways, making the fighter turn the weapon upright in the drawing process. Also, these same steps work with the neck loop carry where the sling is looped around the back of the neck. The weapon hangs up on or off the chest.

The Commando Carry. Horizontal and ready.

Acquisition under combat stress begins.

With a quick and easy lift, fire from the hip or higher position.

The Aussie Quick Draws

Nicknamed in England and the United States the Aussie, since the barrel is pointed down to the other side of the earth, this quick draw is not called this in Australia. Nor is it called the *American* down under. This barrel-down carry is also called the *South African carry,* or just *African* carry, but many soldiers refer to it as an *inclement weather carry,* one that keeps rain or moisture from going down the barrel. The weapon can be shoved back from a horizontal combat position or pitched over your shoulder to attain this barrel-down carry. In the Aussie carry, one must remember to keep the barrel clear of any ground debris. Simply sitting down can project the barrel into whatever is around you.

The barrel-down position can allow for several quick draws under stress. Here are two different kinds of Aussie carries: one with the sling on the same shoulder as the weapon, one where the sling is running over the head on the opposite shoulder, crossing the torso. From these two positions, there are some variables.

Aussie Commando Quick Draw

The sling is wrapped on the strong side shoulder. This carry is obtained by the fighter's commando carry shoved straight back on his back so the barrel is down and the butt is up. Or the commando carry may be shoved all the way over his shoulder until the barrel is pointing downward, butt up.

*Pull the weapon up, while maneuvering your
hands into the shooting position.*

Aussie Quick Draw – The sling and weapon are wrapped on the weak shoulder.

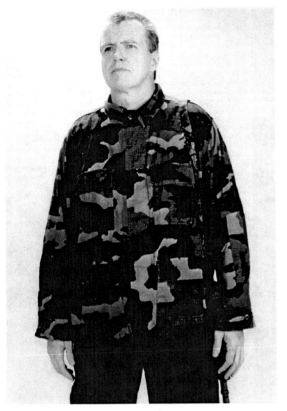 

The Aussie Carry-sling over the weak side shoulder. The same side hand grabs the barrel and lifts the weapon, hopefully to clear the shoulder and any carry gear or epaulets.

With this grip, you raise the weapon barrel forward, turning it counter-clockwise.
Your other hand seeks out the trigger and both hands maneuver the weapon into firing position.

Aussie Cross-Carry Quick Draw – The sling is over the head and on the strong shoulder, weapon hang barrel down on the weak side. This is a very safe and secure way to carry your weapon when you need both for fighting, climbing or other hands free tasks.

Cross carry, an over-the-head sling carry. Same side hand grabs and lifts the weapon.
The other hand snatches the sling and clears the head or any cover (headgear). This step is vital.

You seek the trigger, upright the weapon and fire.

The Combat Re-Sling – Now what if you need your hands to fight, search, climb or downgrade to your pistol? As we did with the pistol, we must do with the long gun. Here is a quick re-sling of your weapon that will place it in a prime position for a future quick draw.

The shooting is over. You need your hands.

Stab your weak hand through the sling. Start ducking. Clear your head and any cover (headgear).

Pitch the weapon over your back. Try to keep the magazine topside for future cross body quick draws. Your hands are free and your weapon is very secure.

Long Gun Quick Draw Summary

The exact scientific breakdown of all these positions and probabilities may be grasped very quickly with just a very short period of practice. Practice these long gun quick draws. See what you may use and then modify them with your body size, equipment and mission. You must also modify your sling as much as possible. My purpose here is to show you the basics and inspire you to customize them to suit your needs, each and every time you step into potential combat. All combat veterans modify and position their gear as their comfort, education, experience and mission demand.

Advanced Multi-Weapon Quick Draws Transitions

It was 1976.

North Koreans killed U.S. Army officers inside the "No Man's Land," of the 49th Parallel. "This is war," our LT told us after an emergency muster, "the highest alarm has sounded." The highest alerts of war were dispatched to us, and I found myself holding an M-16 along with my military police issue .45 semi-auto in a flap holster. I stood in charge of an M-60 team and scanned over rice patties the Red Guard once swarmed some 20 years earlier. On a clear day, atop our SAM missile-laden mountain, with a pair of binoculars we could look north and see the NKs doing jumping jacks in the morning. We were that close.

I suddenly felt the pressing need for extra ammo and a design for combat that included the wisest methods to use both my .45 and my M-16. When the bullets fly, MPs become infantry and in all my basic and advanced training-still of the hard core Vietnam era, the subject of using both these weapons never once came up. Still doesn't. Yet there I was, like so many MPs and other double-armed soldiers before me, armed with both and staring across a potential battlefield. Decades passed, and as a patrolman and a detective all my prowl cars and detective sedans were issued a shotgun, sometimes rifles, for dire calls and arrests. There I was again with two guns in the complete absence of training doctrine.

Decades ago, grunts in combat were often gifted a revolver from home for Christmas, or scavenged one from an enemy stockpile or corpse. Then, as today, elite units usually carried both pistols and shoulder weapons. Modern law enforcement special teams carry both and officers responding to hot situations may pull a shotgun or a police authorized rifle into the fray. A citizen fortunate enough to have a variety of weapons available may need to take action with them on his home ground or community.

When going armed with both a long gun and a pistol, it is wise to practice quick transitions from one to the other and understand when and why such switches are needed. The need to switch weapons may arise from a malfunction, exhausted ammo or an environmental need to change caliber and/or range. I learned the following movements from various U.S. Army Military Police NCOs, and some enlightened civilian police officers that have been in this double-weapon jam before.

Here is some of what I learned from these vets, plus what little I have found in rare doctrine, along with my improvisations I have come to trust. In each scenario you start with a ready weapon with either your pistol up or your rifle up.

Pistol Ready Switch Situation

If your pistol is up and ready, you transition to the long gun for three basic reasons.

> Pistol to Long Gun Transition Reason 1: The pistol is out of ammo.
> Pistol to Long Gun Transition Reason 2: The pistol malfunctions.
> Pistol to Long Gun Transition Reason 3: You need heavier firepower or range.
> Pistol to Long Gun Transition Reason 4: Your pistol is being disarmed from you.

Circumstances like time, ammo and the situation will dictate whether you can keep the pistol on your person for future use or you abandon it under extreme, desperate circumstances.

Rifle Ready Switch Situation

If your long gun is up and ready, you transition to the pistol for five basic reasons.

> Long Gun to Pistol Transition Reason 1: Need lesser firepower
> Long Gun to Pistol Transition Reason 2: The long gun is out of ammunition
> Long Gun to Pistol Transition Reason 3: The long gun malfunctions
> Long Gun to Pistol Transition Reason 4: Need to search tight quarters
> Long Gun to Pistol Transition Reason 5: Your long gun is being disarmed from you

Transition Scenario 1) Alert to Danger or Sudden Very Light Fire – A Sample Study

You search with your pistol and become alerted to serious trouble. Re-holster the pistol while raising the long gun. People with the proper holster and training can holster their handgun with great speed under pressure. However, most do not have such a holster, or such training, and cannot perform this task under heavy combat stress. For the common troop, this process may not be feasible under heavy combat conditions.

You search with a drawn pistol, and detect serious trouble. Long gun kind of trouble.

You holster your weapon and start raising the long gun.

The pistol is back in the holster. Two hands acquire the weapon.

Appropriate action is taken.

Transition Scenario 2) Sudden Light to Medium Fire – A Sample Study

Secure the pistol in your armpit as you raise the long gun. You might have a shoulder holster, but have no time to seat the pistol properly inside it. Instead, quickly tuck your pistol away for heavier fire. In this series, you have emptied your handgun. No time! Tuck it in your armpit.

With the pistol temporarily squeezed in your armpit, take long gun action. Reload, and/or holster your pistol as soon as possible.

Transition Scenario 3) Sudden Heavy Fire – A Sample Study

You might simply drop the pistol and pull up your long gun. For training, have a bean bag chair or large pillow at the range and just drop the pistol into it. Those who say they should never, ever discard their weapon under any circumstances? They simply have never been under extreme heavy fire. Like spent magazines, you may live to recover the weapon as soon as

People who instruct you to NEVER, ever discard your weapon like this, have never felt the stress of enemy gunfire piercing their eardrums.

possible.

The same discarding can be done with the long gun. If you have a sling, the weapon will simply drop to the sling length. Without a sling, the precious weapon will strike the ground. You will have to decide based on the circumstances. These are desperate measures for very desperate times.

Transition Scenario 4) Sudden Heavy Fire – A Sample Study

Count on the sling. If you transition to your pistol from rifle for whatever reason, just as you dropped the pistol, you can drop the long gun to fall sling length and pull the pistol.

Transition Scenario 5) One Finger Span for the Worst Case Scenario – A Sample Study

Long fingers? You need one for this. Under great combat stress, some Vietnam veteran MPs taught me this transition, one originated by sheer, desperate instinct. Let the empty pistol spin loose on your finger as you bring up the long gun and bridge a long trigger finger across the pistol trigger to the trigger of your long gun.

You must practice this with the exact same equipment to see if it works. This transition has been done many times. There are several documented instances I have found where desperate soldiers have shot like this in combat in Africa, the South Pacific and Asia.

As soon as possible, holster the pistol, drop it or use the armpit squeeze. The handgun is a cumbersome burden like this and you must understand this technique is for extreme heavy combat circumstances.

The empty, top-heavy pistol naturally spins, "well-up," and loose on the trigger finger.
The top heavy weight causes the empty handle to flip end up.

The finger crosses the pistol guard and on the long gun trigger, firing the long gun. As soon as possible, do something else with the pistol. Get it off of your trigger finger! This is for dire, temporary emergencies only.

The rare subject of weapon transitions, due to one of your weapons being disarmed and causing you in the process to draw your other weapon, is examined in the disarm module and will be covered in *CQCG Training Mission Four.*

Weapon Transition Summary

From these scenarios, we learn the importance of a sling, a tactical vest clip, maybe even a lanyard for your pistol. Police officers who carry a shotgun or rifle into a conflict without a sling over their shoulder are limiting their options. Soldiers who, in the course of pulling their rifles from shoulder carry positions, and in doing so lose the security of the sling, should re-hook that sling back on the neck and/or shoulder as soon as possible.

Do these simple movements smoothly first, then develop speed. Smooth first, speed second. Do them dry, then start shooting. And then most important, perform them vs. simulated ammo, under some kind of return fire. After all, gunfights are an exchange of rounds. You must master these movements under that stress.

Your Pistol and Long Gun Quick Draw Module
Review and Training Assignment

Practice these draws, drills and scenarios in a hostile environment.
Use loud gunfire sound track, flashing lights and, if in a training room, periods of darkness.

Practice the Quick Draw Positions Solo

QD 1) The Standing QDs

– Draw and shoot from standing triangle grips.
– Draw and shoot from single hand.

QD 2) Knee QDs

– Draw and shoot from double hand grips.
– Draw and shoot from single hand grips.

QD 3) Ground QDs

– Draw and shoot from a forward prone.
– Draw and shoot from a rear prone.

QD 4) Walking Quick Draws

– Draw and shoot from any position.

Practice these responses to attack stimuli with simulated ammunition.

Practice responding to some realistic stimuli with real ammo on a safe range.

Practice the Pistol Quick Draw Drills

Pistol QD Drill 1) Evaluating the two Hand Grip Space Drill

– One Counters QD
– Both armed, do anything

Pistol QD Drill 2) The Space, Stress and Speed Partner Palm Drill

– One Counters QD
– Both armed, do anything

Pistol QD Drill 3) Block, Pass and Pin Drill

        – Shove and quick draw vs. a charging opponent
        – Re-holster! Shove and re-holster

Practice the Combat Scenarios

Pistol QD CS 1) The Interview Stance Sets

        – push and draw
        – block and draw
        – strike and draw

Pistol QD CS 2) Countering the CQC Pistol to Throat Threat

Pistol QD CS 3) Countering the Rifle Snapshooter

Pistol QD CS 4) Countering the Ground Knife Attacker

Pistol QD CS 5) Left Hand Quick Draw

Practice Rifle Quick Draws from Shoulder Sling Carries

Rifle QD 1) From the GI Carry

Rifle QD 2) Commando QD

Rifle QD 3) Aussie QD

        – single shoulder carry
        – cross back carry

Rifle QD 4) Rifle Combat Re-sling

Practice the Weapon Transition Quick Draws

WP 1) Pistol to Rifle

WP 2) Rifle to Pistol

CQCG

Introduction to Knife Fighting
The Knife Combat Quick Draw Module

Introduction: The Numbers of the Knife

A Knife/Counter-Knife Combatives course must be a broad, sweeping study. The following is my personal course outline I use to organize the tactics and strategies required for such a comprehensive foundation. Here is the science of how I *run the numbers of the knife.*

Two Types of Knives

There are fixed-blade knives and folding knives. Fixed blades are edged weapons that are a solid piece from blade tip to handle, or are in essence non-foldable. Folding knives bend at a designated point. There are two kinds of folding knives, utility and tactical. Utility knives are worker's tools and general purpose pocket knives. Tactical knives are really designed to be fighting knives under the guise of the term *tactical.*

> Knife Type 1) Fixed-blade knives
> Knife Type 2) Folding knives
>
> > – Utility/work folders
> > – Tactical folders

Three Knife Carry Sites

A carry site is military and police jargon for where someone stores their weapon on or near their body. There are primary carry sites for quick draw access, secondary carry sites for back-up weapons and tertiary "lunge and reach" sites where an opponent can reach and snatch a weapon. Watch the hands. It is the hands that will kill you.

> Carry Site 1) Primary sites (for quick draws)
> Carry Site 2) Secondary sites (for back-up)
> Carry Site 3) Lunge and reach sites (for both)

Two Reasons to Quick Draw

The practice of drawing your weapon under combat stress is important. You pull your knife and gun to present the weapon to prevent violence before it happens. You also pull your knife during violence as a tool to stop the violence.

> Quick Draw Reason 1) Pre-preemptive. To present to prevent violence.
> Quick Draw Reason 2) To put an end to the violence while it is underway.

Two Target Profiles

You will engage in knife combat with only two groups, the enemy soldier and the criminal.

> Target Profile 1) Enemy soldiers
> Target Profile 2) Criminals

Two Use of Force Results

Combat results in either lethal or less-than-lethal ends. Sometimes we must control, contain and/or arrest the enemy. Sometimes we must kill them. How do you decide to conduct lethal or less-than-lethal combat? You must plan your combat action on moral, ethical and legal considerations of the predicament in which you find yourself.

> Use of Force 1) Lethal
> Use of Force 2) Less-than-lethal

Four Knife Assault Tools

You can use the tip, the edge, the pommel and the flat of the blade to fight.

> Tool 1) Tip for stabbing
> Tool 2) Edges for slashing
> Tool 3) Flats for impacts
> Tool 4) Pommel (or unopened folder) for impact strikes

Four Basic Knife Grips

You will either be right-handed, left-handed, in a saber grip or reverse grip. The saber and reverse grips have sub-categories depending upon the position of the thumb, the ball of the thumb and the cant of the wrist.

> Basic Knife Grip 1) Right-handed
> Basic Knife Grip 2) Left-handed
> Basic Knife Grip 3) Saber Grip
> Basic Knife Grip 4) Reverse Grip

Six Knife Fighting Positions

A fighting stance is really nothing more than athletic balance and strength in motion, but there are three primary standing positions. One is knife forward. The second is knife back, and the third is knife neutral, near your side. Make no mistake, you will quickly transition through these in the maneuvers of real combat. There is simply no one perfect fighting stance, no matter what source or expert you may hear proclaiming an ultimate stance. There are three primary ground fighting positions-knee high, on your back, or on your sides. A consummate knife fighting trainer practices equally in all six of these positions because in the chaos of combat he may well have to fight in all of these positions.

     Position 1) Standing and knife forward
     Position 2) Standing and knife neutral (not forward or back)
     Position 3) Standing and knife back
     Position 4) Knee high on one or two knees
     Position 5) Down on your back
     Position 6) Down on either your right or left sides

Position 1) Standing and knife forward.

Position 2) Standing and knife neutral.

Position 3) Standing and knife rear.

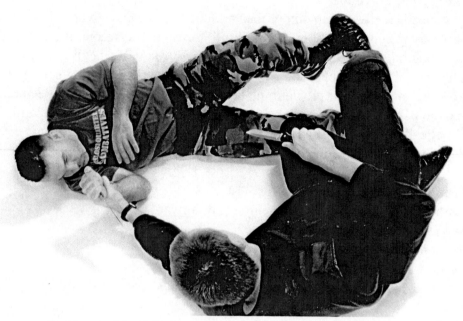

Position 6 of the 6) *Fighting down and on either your right or left side.*

Two Ranges of Knife Combat

Dueling and close quarters are the two major knife ranges of defined knife combat. Throwing a knife, a theoretic third range, is a risky, really questionable strategy. Some systems worry enough to divide the CQC confrontation into more ranges of mere inches, but that is space covered in milli-seconds of combat. Entirely too much knife training time is spent on dueling, a range least likely to occur in modern combat. Many knife fights begin and end on the ground, or inside places like cars, etc.

> Range 1) Dueling range
> Range 2) CQC range, where the limbs could be grabbed

Two Points of Knife Combat Contact

The enemy will either make first contact upon you with his knife, or make his first contact upon you with his limb with strikes, grabs or wraps, and then use the knife. Your combat scenario training should cover both of these basic possibilities.

> Contact Point 1) Enemy knife makes first contact
> Contact Point 2) Enemy limb makes first contact, then the knife contacts

Two Assault "Speeds"

The enemy will attack you with an emotional over-thrust that may offer an extended arm and great energy, or he will attack you with a pumping arm-not unlike a balanced boxer.

> Assault Speed 1) Emotional over-extension
> Assault Speed 2) Pumping motion

Six Knife Assault Drills

You must practice saber grip slashing, reverse grip slashing, hacking, saber grip stabbing, reverse grip stabbing and pommel striking in standing, kneeling and ground positions to be a consummate practitioner. The pommel striking must also include the use of a folding knife as a palm stick (essentially two pommels). A knife expert is well versed in all six.

Assault 1) Saber slashing
Assault 2) Reverse slashing
Assault 3) Hacking
Assault 4) Reverse grip stabbing
Assault 5) Saber grip stabbing
Assault 6) Pommel strikes

Three Counters to Common Blocks

You attack. He blocks. Interrupted, you can pursue three main strategies. One is cut the block. Or, you can redirect the knife to another line of attack. You can also invade/trap the block.

Counter 1) Cut the block.
Counter 2) Redirect your knife onto another line of attack.
Counter 3) Invading hands – trap the block.

Four Basic Invading/Trapping Hands

Getting into closer quarters, you can use the *four P's*. Pin, Pass, Pull or Push the opponent's limbs to get a better target. This is the simple essence of trapping. The enemy's arms are mere obstructions to a better target.

Invasion 1) Pin (or wrap) the obstructing arm.
Invasion 2) Pass the obstructing arm.
Invasion 3) Pull the obstructing arm.
Invasion 4) Push the obstructing arm.

Five Obstacles to Victory

Your knife must overcome the opponent's mental and physical condition, plus the clothing he wears.

Obstacle 1) His size, strength and condition
Obstacle 2) His arms up and in the way
Obstacle 3) His sudden, explosive and reflexive body movements
Obstacle 4) His clothing
Obstacle 5) His adrenaline

One Unarmed Combatives Course
Too often, naive knife practitioners knife fight as though the conflict were a fencing match. They end their scenarios with a simple stab. A stab or a slash or two, like fists and bullets, are notorious for not finishing a fight. You must develop unarmed striking, blocking, kicking, take-downs, throws, and ground fighting in a highly combative, non-sport, cheating course to support your knife action. Overuse the knife, but support the knife with your body.

Three Angles of Attack Drills
These three cover all the essentials of slashing, stabbing, pommel striking and training.

        Angle of Attack Drill 1) 8 angles of slashing
        Angle of Attack Drill 2) 10 angles of stabbing
        Angle of Attack Drill 3) 12 angles for training a partner's responses

The Knife Quick Draw Module

Knife QD Studies and Observations 1) The Sheaths, Clips and Carries of the Knife

I will not bore you with the typical product, catalog line that makes up most knife books. A sheath will hold a fixed and folding knife in primary and secondary carry sites. Knives without sheaths rest in carry places like pockets.

The manufactured location of carry clips on folding knives are almost always very restrictive, limiting a right or left-handed person to only certain ways to pull and open the knife, despite their desired saber or reverse grip. The very best folding knives allow for a clip to be positioned on any one of the four corners of the folded knife. This allows a person to customize their knife for a right or left-side carry to produce a saber or reverse grip.

It might sound extreme, but it is wise to carry at least two knives. One on each side of your body. This affords you access to one should you be ground fighting, carrying a firearm on your strong side, or even bitten by a dog with a death grip on your forearm – anything that restricts acquiring a knife carried on one side only.

Knife QD Studies and Observations 2) The Stealth Quick Draw

In certain situations, people can predict trouble. *The best weapon quick draw is always the one that has the weapon out and ready before the physical incident.* Some circumstances require a stealth, or quiet acquisition to make-ready the folding knife. The typical metallic snap of a blade popping into place is a telltale sound to a potential enemy. Study and practice with your knife. Learn its *seating* mechanism. Is there a tension bar? A lock? How does the blade lock into place? If you suddenly flick it into position, you will hear its quick draw sound.

Once you discover how your knife functions, see how you can make the blade seat into position without creating that sound. Usually this means depressing the seating mechanism.

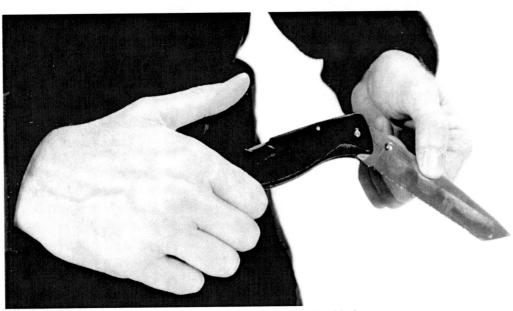

Step 1) *Partially open the blade.*

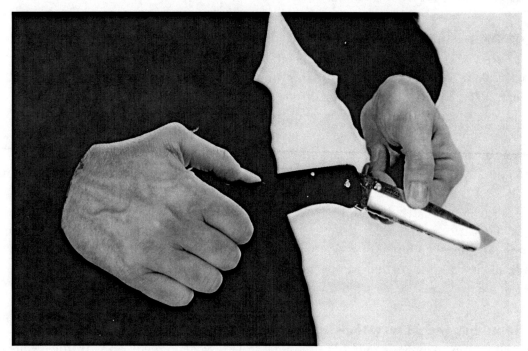

Step 2) *Depress the mechanism that will eventually lock the blade into place.*

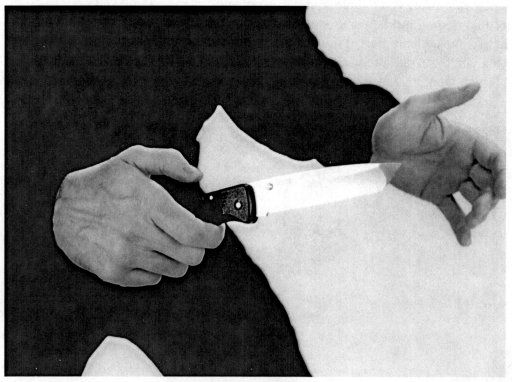

Step 3) *Place the blade into position, and then release your depression upon the locking mechanism. You have quietly opened your knife without alerting potential enemies.*

Knife Quick Draw Studies and Observations 3) Barney and the Two Jacks

In our study progression we have developed the quick draw with firearms and now the knife. Many of the same strategies and tactics apply. At some point our knife is drawn either for a presentation to prevent violence before it starts, or to stop violence while it is happening. We will start with the subject of presentation.

"The mightiest warrior never has to use his sword," is an old martial arts expression. This plays to the reputation of a person. Combine that with a solid command presence and you lesson the chance of having to fight. Many researchers say a message is 90 percent non-verbal and 10 percent verbal and constructing that 100 percent is a vital fighting strategy. Review again my litany of *Barney and the Two Jacks*.

If you must quick draw a weapon to shut down possible violence or interrupt violence, your bluff must be effective, and you must have a command presence. If Mayberry PD's Barney Fife draws down on a killer, his shaking voice and hand will convince the suspect he has a chance that Barney will not use his weapon and could be overcome. If Jack Webb draws down on a killer, his dedication to rules is a tip-off to the killer that Webb may be pushed and toyed with for a chance to escape, especially if the killer is unarmed. There is little chance Jack Webb will make good his threat to stab or shoot an unarmed man. If Jack Nicholson draws down on a killer, in fine "Here's Johnny!" fashion, the killer will realize this Jack is crazed and is liable to twist off and kill him for little to no reason. Which method of acting would you use to bluff? You do not have to assume the complete Jack Nicholson persona, but find one and practice it.

There is a school of thought that states you should not threaten the enemy with something that you cannot actually do. But this destroys the trick bluff, the Jack Nicholson threat, and that threat has frozen many in their tracks and has worked hundreds of thousands of times in civilian, military and enforcement situations. If the bluff doesn't work? At least you tried! Take a deep breath, holster/sheath up and go do what you've got to do next.

Knife Quick Draw Synergy Drills

Knife QD Drill 1) Learn Your Knife

Solo command and mastery of the quick draw. Practice your quick draw. Practice getting your knife out of its carry site and opening it up. Practice it standing, kneeling and on the ground. Get the feel of your knife. Make sure it has a textured handle to improve your grip. Sweat and blood on the handle will cause slippage. Of course the best combat knives open by spring mechanisms, but are illegal in most cities, states and many countries. Smooth first, speed later. This learning process also develops the quick draw for that *presentation* to scare off potential violence.

Knife QD Drill 2) The 12 Angle Knife Quick Draw Assault Drill

Now quick draw your knife into action. You should be able to draw and attack in a number of angles. The 12 angle training drill, used throughout the CQCG course material is an excellent way to develop this skill. At this level of command and mastery we introduce the drill. These should be practiced standing, kneeling and on the ground. Practice these right and left-handed, saber or reverse grip. This format below is diagramed for the right-handed. Just reverse the order for left-handed grips. Each time, re-sheath or close up the knife and put it back in your carry site.

The 12 Angles are:

Angle 1: Inward slash from the high right
Angle 2: Backhanded slash from the high left
Angle 3: Inward slash from the low right
Angle 4: Backhanded slash from the low left
Angle 5: Stomach stab
Angle 6: Left chest stab
Angle 7: Right chest stab
Angle 8: Backhanded thigh high slash
Angle 9: Inward thigh high slash
Angle 10: Inward eye-high hook stab
Angle 11: Backhanded eye-high hook stab
Angle 12: Downward slash

The training insert variations are:

Grip variables
  – Saber Grip
  – Reverse Grip
  – Right-handed
  – Left-handed

Position variables
  – Standing
  – Kneeling
  – On your back
  – On your side

Resistance variables
  – In the air
  – Against a training post to feel the gravitas of a real target

(This angle drill is demonstrated in numerous Hochheim training videos.)

Knife QD Drill 3) Shaving Time Off of the Draw

You pull the knife, your finger indexing whatever disc, opening or device that helps open the blade. You open the knife about three-quarters of the way and let the momentum of your primary attack seat and lock the blade in place.

You see the need to draw.

You access the knife.

You access the blade opening mechanism.

You open the blade...

...about three-quarters of the way.

Attack! The slashing energy seats the blade.

Smooth first. Speed later. There are also times of extreme close quarters when your quick draw process, especially while opening a folder is easily countered. Under these circumstances, protect the process by opening the knife behind your leg.

Knife QD Drill 4) Cue Drills

As we progress toward interaction with a training partner, we have a trainer standing before the trainee. He executes some cue for the trainee to quick draw the knife. Make sure your cues are realistic, such as the actual physical action of an opponent pulling his knife.

Cue Drill 1) Stand and draw on cue.

Cue Drill 2) Walk and draw on cue.

Cue Drill 3) Ground QDs – the trainer stands before a downed trainee and circles the trainee. On cue, the trainee must draw from a ground position.

Knife QD Drill 5) Focus Mitt Drills

As we progress further toward interaction with a training partner, we have a trainer standing before the trainee. He produces a training pad for the trainee to quick draw the knife and strike the pad.

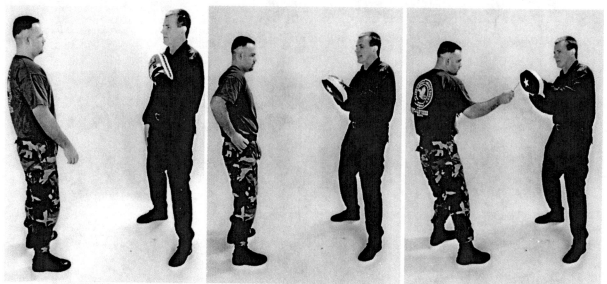

Train with a variety of targets at heights and angles that develop stabbing and slashing skills.

There is an art and science to properly presenting the focus mitt to a trainee, whether you are developing the boxer, the stick or knife fighter. Give clear and obvious target opportunities. The smaller pads and focus mitts worked on your hands and forearms are first and foremost, about target acquisition and speed, not necessarily power. The bigger the pad, the more the power. The faster you flash the mitt, the faster the trainee will have to strike out. This develops great speed.

You can also strike a stick controlled by a trainer. The trainer will feed the stick to you in ways similar to the focus mitt.

Knife QD Drill 6) The Two Hand Space Awareness Drill

Two training partners stand facing each other, one arm length apart. The trainee has a training weapon in his or her quick draw carry site. The trainer is unarmed. The purpose of the drill is to teach physical distance awareness. The trainer plans to interrupt the trainee's quick draw. How far away can an enemy be before the trainee can successfully draw the fixed blade, or draw and open a folded knife?

Increase the distance with experimentation. This is nothing but a space and speed awareness drill. After a series of experiments, the trainee will have a working knowledge of when a edged weapon quick draw might be safely achieved.

This is also not the time to construct elaborate counters to quick draws scenarios. We will be doing those in later levels as we develop more unarmed combatives skills. This is to teach the trainee what it takes to quick draw his or her knife and see how much distance and support methods may be needed. Your support hand may clear a path or buy a few seconds for a quick draw. In extreme close quarters it is good to blade your body weapon-side back to protect your quick draw process. In essence, this looks in a still photograph to be a knife-back stance. I remind you that there is no perfect so-called stance.

Knife QD Drill 7) Basic Stand-Off Quick Draw

This drill is strictly for awareness and experience. Two training partners, both armed with knives in carry sites, stand a few feet apart. They press palm to palm. Either one suddenly tries to quick draw their knife. The process is enlightening. They see who can draw first, but this study goes deeper.

Strictly for speed and space awareness, this drill forces a person to understand the mechanical process involved with opening a folding knife under attack stress.

Round 1: Both armed and quick draw.
Round 2: One armed and one unarmed. Unarmed tries to disrupt the QD.
Round 3: Both armed again-this time wiser.

By Round 3, fresh from the results from Round 2 where they charged in and countered the draw, they must make an educated choice to draw or charge in to counter their opponent's quick draw. This is a fantastic drill to gauge space, speed, options and response.

Sometimes the support arm may be injured in this quick draw drill. There is much to learn in this practice session.

Knife QD Drill 8) CQC Flow Drill

Using the staple Block, Pass and Pin six count/beat drill diagramed earlier in this book; attempt quick draws on some of the half beats. Some half-beats work with same-side pulls, some with cross-draws. Remember these drills because later in the CQCG course we will use them to learn how to counter knife quick draws. As you view these pictures, remember how each step progresses. You are interrupting the six beat drill diagramed earlier in this book. The trainee is dealing with an incoming attack of some type. In this series you will interrupt the pattern after step/beat 3 with a stress quick draw.

Step/Beat 1: A reflexive block
Step/Beat 2: A passing over of the attack
Step/Beat 3: A pinning push
Step/Beat 3 1/2: A quick draw while pushing the enemy's limb
Step/Beat 4: Any counter attack

Try the same movements vs. a stick attack. On Step/Beat 3 1/2 control the weapon-bearing limb long enough to get that knife up and out.

Allow yourself time to draw and open that folder.
Take immediate action.

Try the same movement vs. a reverse grip knife attack.

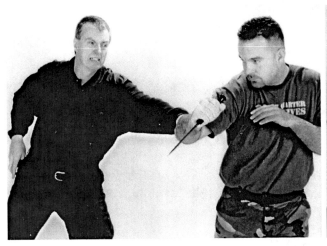

Variation 1) Have the trainer charge right back to interrupt the quick draw.

Variation 2) Grab the limb on first contact, strike the face, then quick draw.

Variation 3) Carry your weapon in a different place and attempt quick draws on differing 1/2 beats.

Variation 4) Experiment with the trainee down and on his back.

Variation 5) Continue to develop your own variations.

A multitude of action follow-ups will be taught in the upcoming *CQCG Training Mission* books. This mission is primarily to instruct the information surrounding quick draws.

Knife QD Drill 9) The Ground Roll Knife Rattlesnake Drill

Again we use the ground roll format. Start in any ground position and assign the trainee to quick draw and slash and/or stab when possible. The trainee must pull his knife under this stress. An unforgettable practice.

In this position don't forget the knee strikes, or more specifically in this case "thigh" strikes that may stun, unbalance and upset the attacker.

Do not end the practice in one stab or slash. Make the trainer fight you long enough to simulate a successful, real world counter-attack.

    Round 1) The trainer does not specifically interfere with the actual quick draw. He just fights as he would if the opponent was unarmed.

    Round 2) The trainer tries specifically to interrupt the knife quick draw.

    Round 3) Both the trainer and the trainee have knives. They quick draw as well as try to interrupt each other's quick draw as they see fit.

    Here we will introduce a less-than-lethal option, one that we will study extensively in future ***CQCG Training Mission*** books. You pulled your knife. Perhaps, due to the configuration of your struggle, your enemy doesn't see you have a knife, or perhaps he sees it. Taking the tip and pressing it against his body, like his throat or even ribs, and issuing a *surrender or die death threat* may cause him to stand down.

Knife Quick Draw Option Awareness Combat Scenarios

KQD CS 1) The Interview Stance Series – Sample Studies

In the gun quick draw chapter of this book, we explained the interview stance, that calm-looking, unoffensive, torso bladed position taken just a step out of the range of a suspicious person in front of you. Unlike a pistol, a quick draw from a knife may take a few extra steps. Few fixed blade sheaths are made for quick draws. Tactical folders need to be opened. All this may require more shield time with your free hand, and/or footwork.

1a) The Push or Strike Quick Draw Practice. In a pre-preemptive attack, or a defensive move as an opponent rushes you, you push and draw from your primary carry site, follow-up as needed. This same motion is similar to a backhand or forearm strike.

1b) The Block and Quick Draw Practice

KQD Combat Scenario 2) Counter the Rear Choke – A Sample Study

Practice this one. The object is to stab the leg of the attacker, matching the same side as the arm that is choking you. This should earn a release, as you will see in this step-by-step study.

WARNING! DO NOT STAB OR SLASH BACK IN THE DIRECTION OF YOUR OWN THROAT! In really violent attacks, the assailant usually hauls and wrestles you around, making such arm attacks very dangerous.

DO NOT DO THIS!

He gets a choke or at least a neck restraint on you. You try the trick of buying a few seconds by maneuvering inside the arm. You are thinking first of your knife for defense.

Once you have drawn and opened the folder, you attack the right leg if the right arm is used to choke or restrain you. This may involve switching hands.

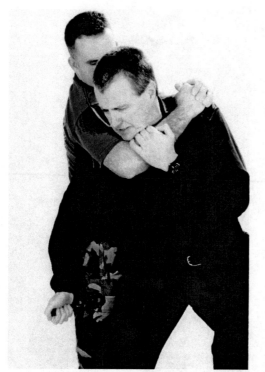

Common sense tells us that after severely stabbing and ripping this thigh, the attacker will usually reflexively try to make the pain and destruction stop. He will release the grip and try to catch your weapon bearing limb.

There are several options at this point, but one is to turn around and bash his throat with the most powerful strike you can muster. Bash and bash as needed.

Chokes, neck restraints and counters will be studied extensively in **CQCG Training Mission Six.**

KQD Combat Scenarios 3) Tactical Folder for Handgun Retention – Sample Studies

When an enforcement officer loses his or her pistol, they are usually shot and killed by their own gun, at the hands of the person who disarmed them. This is a life or death situation. There are no current statistics on civilian concealed carry disarms and shootings, but anyone can see how grave the situation might be. If you are fighting for your gun, you are fighting for your life.

3a) The Efficient Path
When your gun is grabbed, you quick draw your weak side carry knife and stab the throat.

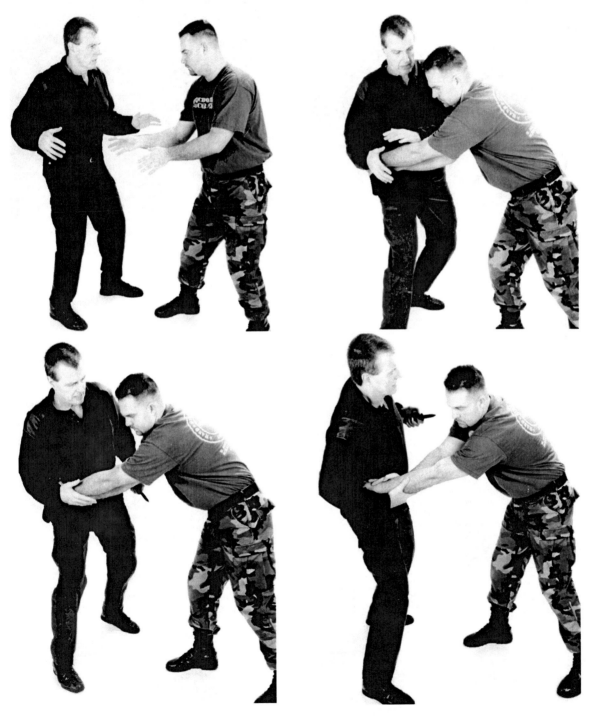

You will attack directly, and you will stay on the attack until you are sure the death threat has ended.

Bang those arms away!

Many veterans will admit that once their weapon has been grabbed, they clamp down with their elbow and lock on with their hands. They turn away from the enemy, their weapon-side back. All good initial reflexes. Once this first response has been established, you must counter attack. A knife is an efficient and appropriate weapon for such times.

All personnel and civilians should be armed with a knife in this day and age of a vast variety of models and sizes.

I have created an extensive, scientific training module on handgun retention, which will appear in *CQCG Training Mission Five*. One tool is the use of the folding knife.

3b) Arms Away First!

This time your quick draw arm bashes the attacker's arms. This may or may not garner a release, so you must act accordingly.

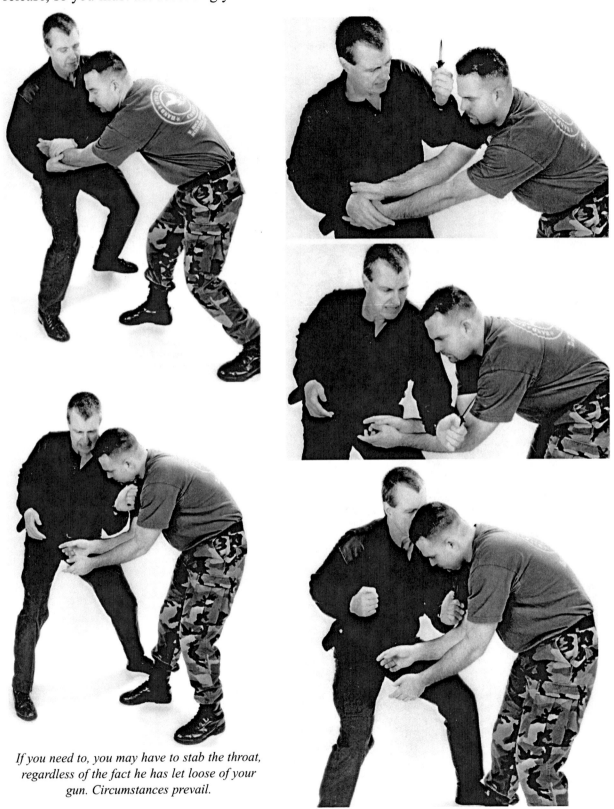

If you need to, you may have to stab the throat, regardless of the fact he has let loose of your gun. Circumstances prevail.

KQD Combat Scenario 4) The Ground Quick Draw – Sample Studies

This is exactly like the stress pistol quick draw demonstrated in the previous chapter. Review that section. It starts with the worst case problem – a knifer on top. You push hard, get and go with the reverse energy, then splay out. In one set, he lets go and catches himself. In the other set, he retains a grip on your weapon-side arm. You duck under, bridge against the arm and pull your hand free. Both sets end with counter-attacks to finish the fight.

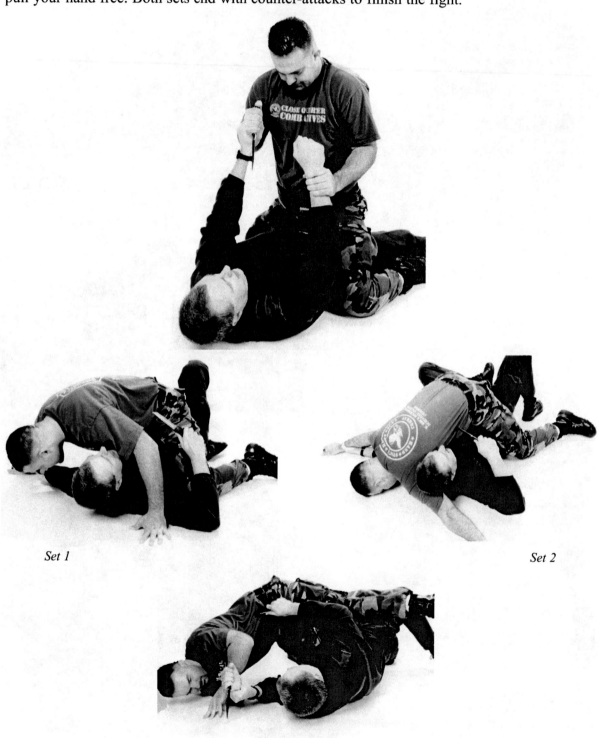

Set 1

Set 2

ALWAYS

Always use your environment, trickery and deception. Always!
Cheat first! Cheat last!
Cheat in the middle.

Your Knife Quick Draw Module Review and Assignment

Practice the Knife Quick Draw Positions

KQD 1) The Standing QDs.

- Solo
- With mitts, pads, and solid posts

KQD 2) Walking Quick Draws

Practice the Quick Draw Drills

KQD Drill 1) Evaluating the Space Drill

KQD Drill 2) Partner Palm Drill

- Both QD
- One Counters QD
- Both Armed, do anything

KQD Drill 3) Block, Pass and Pin Drill

- Shove and quick draw
- Shove and quick draw – the trainer charges back to interrupt

Practice the Option Awareness Combat Scenarios

KQD CS 1) The Interview Stance Sets

- Push and draw
- Block and draw
- Strike and draw

QD CS 2) Countering the Neck Choker

QD CS 3) Tactical Folder for Handgun Retention

QD CS 4) Countering the Ground Knife Attacker

CQCG

Introduction to SDMS
The Impact Weapon Quick Draw Module

SDMS is both a single-handed and double-handed tactical impact weapon conflict system broken down in two reference/study categories of SMS and DMS. DMS is double-handed grip tactics and strategies. Together they comprise SDMS. These two parts are interchangeable while in conflict. SMS is a single-handed or solo hand grip tactics and strategies. They are largely taught in an integrated format because the practitioner must be able to transition to both hand grips as needed while in conflict. Several of the tactics are inspired from Spanish and Filipino maneuvers, thus the Spanish word for hand, *manos,* is used in the course title.

SMS: Solo Manos (hand) System – single-hand grip tactics.
DMS: Double or Dos Manos (hand) System – double-hand grip tactics.

SDMS is developed for the seamless application of all single-handed and double-handed grip, impact weapon tactics in all ranges of standing, kneeling and ground fighting close quarter combat.

SDMS instructs the entire spectrum of conflict from visual presence to deadly force as legally needed. SDMS is structured to educate the practitioner in visual, audible and physical impact weapon tactics and strategies through the following process.

Concealed impact weapon strategies

Impact weapon presentations and verbal commands to quell conflicts

Impact weapon tactics and strategies to move opposing personnel

Impact weapon tactics and strategies to control and contain opposing personnel

Impact weapon and bayonet tactics and strategies to fight against deadly threats

Impact weapon retention to prevent disarming

Impact weapon tactics that relate to long guns

Unarmed tactics and strategies vs. SDMS attackers

SDMS impact weapons or long weapons include the following:

The martial arts stick or cane

The enforcement night stick

The side-handle enforcement night stick

The walking and/or hiking cane

The tactical flashlight

The expandable baton

The riot baton

The umbrella

The rifle

The shotgun

The machine gun

The bayoneted long gun

DMS tactics and strategies relate directly to rifle and bayonet techniques.

SDMS material finds its sources in:

Military

Law Enforcement

Security

Pacific Island Martial Arts
  – Japan
  – Philippines
  – Indonesia
  – Hawaii

Hybrid Martial Systems

SDMS Studies and Observations 1) Selecting your Weapon

Weapon Selection 1) Mission needs

In the 1960's in the United States, protesters called the M-16 armed military's bluff at Kent State University and were shot, causing great turmoil in society. Carrying an M-16 to quell some disturbances can be a mistake. The employment of less-than-lethal tools would be smarter. Define your mission. Predict your problems. Sometimes a long flashlight is all that's required, sometimes the smallest expandable baton.

Weapon Selection 2) Your body size, strength and shape

This will dictate the type of weapon you select and your skill at manipulating it. The weapon needs to be long enough to be an effective crowbar for leverage with two hands, yet short enough for you to execute all your single-handed tactics.

A common walking cane or the martial arts stick are impact weapons, as is any object of appropriate length.

This Frankfurt, Germany police stick was given to me after teaching their Frankfurt SWAT team. As you can see, it is very short and made of a very hard rubber.

Expandable batons come in a variety of sizes. These three are the typical sizes from 12 inches to 28 inches.

There are belt holsters available that adjust for a vertical to horizontal carry. Th model shown here also has a side-break-away release. This allows for both a drawing pull-out quick draw and side break pull-out. One thing to consider, the average dress belt that a plainclothes officer or civilian might wear will not successfully support the weapon or be strong enough to handle the break-away action.

SDMS Studies and Observations 2) The Impact Weapon Grips
The SDMS course covers all the single-handed and double-handed grips on all impact weapons.
All too often most of these grips are completely ignored, omitting vital life-saving strategies.

        SDMS Grip 1) SMS single-hand end grip
                1a) Saber
                1b) Reverse Grip

        SDMS Grip 2) SMS single-hand Center Grip

        SDMS Grip 3) DMS double-hand Sword Grip, a modified sports bat or sword grip

        SDMS Grip 4) DMS double-hand grip
                4a) Rifle Grip-one palm up, one palm down
                4b) Stick Grip-both palms down

        SDMS Grip 5) Hybrid grips for certain uniquely shaped, impact weapons

Photo Displays of Each SMS and DMS Grip:

Grip 1a) SMS: The standard, popular one-hand grip, saber-style.   *Grip 1b) SMS: The single-handed, reverse grip.*

Grip 2) SMS: *The Center Grip, a one-handed, choked up hold in or near the middle of the weapon.*

Grip 3) DMS: *The common baseball bat grip. Note the space between the hands. As with a katana (sword), this offers more control.*

Grip 4a) DMS: *The stick grip with both palms down.*

Grip 4b) DMS: *The rifle grip, one palm up, one palm down.*

Grip 5) DMS: Hybrid Grip – A Sample. *This is when two hands control an impact weapon that is shaped in a manner other than a straight, slick weapon.*

Impact Weapon Studies and Observations 3) Carry and Ready-to-Draw Positions

Impact weapons come in fixed sizes carried and/or concealed where possible on the body. Expandable batons are compressed and carried usually in pockets or holsters. Here are some side carries, cross draw carries and hybrid carries.

Right-on right, strong side belt carry.

Right-to-left, weak side carry.

A *strong-side* is defined as the strong and/or dominant hand. *Weak-side* is the opposite. Citizens, soldiers and enforcement personnel will carry their impact weapons where needed or required. People wearing handguns will often carry their impact weapon on the non-gun side. People prohibited from carrying firearms will carry their impact weapons on their strong side. As with the handgun and knife, think of the three carry sites:

1) Primary – think quick draw
2) Secondary – think back-up
3) Lunge and Reach – think off the body locations

Impact Weapon Studies and Observations 3) Quick Draw Mechanics
As with the pistol and knife, getting your impact weapon up and out for the fight is one of the most over-looked and unemphasized practices. You will be faced with:

QD 1) Drawing your fixed weapon from your strong side or weak side.
QD 2) Drawing and opening an expandable baton with momentum.
QD 3) Drawing and opening an expandable baton with two hands.

Walk softly but carry a baseball bat. To the left I have a Louisville Slugger in my left pocket. A bouncer in Great Britain showed me this one. Below, see how he carried a little league baseball bat under his suit coat when walking around on dangerous nights. Normal dress pants with deep pockets do the job. No sitting down though!

Fixed stick quick draw from a belt carry. This reverse grip grab leads off with a pommel thrust to an enemy. This is an example of a fixed quick draw that doesn't require a lot of arm space.

Retaining the Baton: Countering Your Interrupted Belt-Carry Quick Draw

Many police officers, military personnel and security officers carry batons. Many are issued "straight," simple sticks that are carried on their uniform belts in partial leather holsters, or hung by rings on straps. If the officer carries a pistol on his strong side, he will carry his baton on his weak side. Many officers and guards around the world do not carry firearms and are issued impact weapons. In this case, these non-firearm personnel will carry their sticks on their strong side.

The Belt Carry Quick Draws:

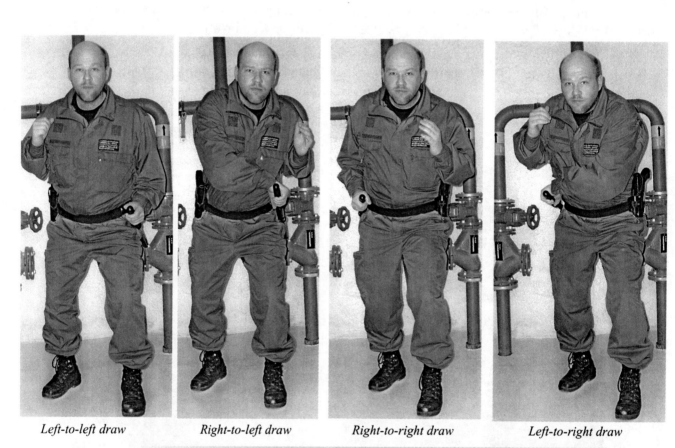

Left-to-left draw   Right-to-left draw   Right-to-right draw   Left-to-right draw

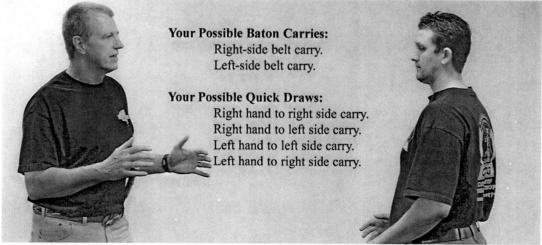

Your Possible Baton Carries:
Right-side belt carry.
Left-side belt carry.

Your Possible Quick Draws:
Right hand to right side carry.
Right hand to left side carry.
Left hand to left side carry.
Left hand to right side carry.

Here is a momentum quick draw of an expandable baton. This one needs whipping strength and enough space for the telescopic action to lock into place. As with the knife quick draw previously shown, you may sometimes get the lock in place as you deliver the first strike.

Draw and extend the expandable baton. The momentum expansion: One sample.

Pull apart expansion by hand to a locked position for larger, heavier models: A sample.

Impact Weapon Studies and Observations 4) Understanding Public Perception

You have drawn your weapon. You have done this to create a command presence to stop violence before it happens, or to stop violence while it is happening. People around you will be witnesses for or against your actions, all viewing the events through their prejudices and memories. Many legal experts say that while in action you should say things like:

> *"Stop! Do not make me hurt you."*
> *"I do not want to hurt you."*

If you are a true, mature student of modern, survival strategies, then you must recognize all the post-action challenges that arise. You must survive this aftermath. All your actions must be appropriate legal, moral, ethical use of force considerations.

Impact Weapon Studies and Observations 5) Pre-Fight and Ready Positions

Whether you are a citizen, or uniformed personnel, your command presence, from the second you arrive on the scene to how you begin to fight, is important. FBI "Officer Killed" surveys that interviewed cop-killers and muggers, rapists and robbers learn that they size-up their intended victims well before attacking them. A person's appearance, bearing and behavior strongly influence their opponents. Citizens, soldiers and officers who look out of shape, slovenly, and seem to show a lack of skill or confidence are likely to become targets. Review the *Barney and the Two Jacks* essay that appears in a previous chapter.

Here are the major drawn positions and pre-fight stances.

Parade Rest 1) The Quad Rest *– weapon rests across both front thighs.*

Parade Rest 2) Ham Rest *– weapon rests across both rear thighs.*

The Classic Port Arms *– the on-guard position.*

The two *Parade Rest* positions shown above are considered *stand-down* poses and are taught to law enforcement, corrections and military personnel that are expected to face crowd and riot control problems. They are somewhat aggressive in the view of a crowd, in that an impact weapon is out and ready. Yet, is not up, as in the port arms position shown here to the left, or reared back and about to strike.

These differing postures are important tactics when attempting to manage the moods and actions of a potentially hostile crowd. Material concerning riot control strategies and tactics will appear in ***CQCG Training Mission Ten.***

SMS Saber Grip – bladed and hidden behind leg.　　　*SMS Reverse Grip – hidden behind the back.*

When dealing with the Japanese style *tonfa* stick shown below, the extra side handle can be used as either an up-grip or a down-grip. This allows for a powerful thrusting action, but the handle does little else, and for myself and many experts fully trained in the potential of the simple stick, the right-angle side handle seems to get in the way of a multitude of superior tactics. Striking using the handle as a pivot point while the short shaft strikes in a fanning motion, is very lame. It looks brutal to the naive witness, but does little impact damage to the subject.

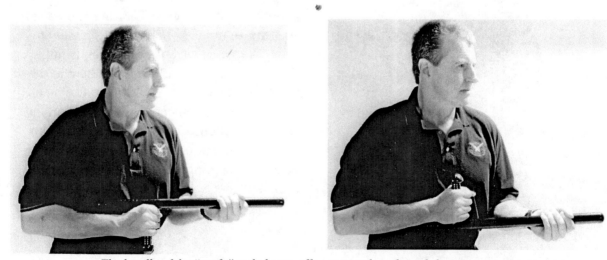

The handle of the "tonfa" style baton offers tremendous frontal thrusting power.
But that is about all the handle is good for.

All impact weapon training must include equal amounts of knee-high and ground fighting tactics and strategies. Two-handed DMS movements often directly relate to staff fighting tactics. Also, a stick makes an excellent combat companion with a knife.

The so-called *fighting stance* varies also as needed, from concealed positions to stand-down positions to conflict positions. Through it all a certain body balance, whether standing still or in motion, needs to be maintained. Maximum mobility with balance and power is vital. There are six basic, aggressive impact weapon conflict positions to train in:

1) Stick held forward, the other hand up and ready
2) Stick held neutral, near the hip, the other hand up and ready
3) Stick held back, the other hand up and ready
4) Knee-high: on your knee or knees
5) On your back
6) On your sides

Impact Weapon Quick Draw Synergy Drills

When you consider the variables involved with the carry and quick draw of an impact weapon, it becomes more difficult to create a few main training drills for all the following factors.

Factor 1) Fixed sticks of varying lengths
Factor 2) Expandable batons of varying lengths
Factor 3) Belt carries with break away holsters or ring straps
Factor 4) Momentum openings for expandable batons
Factor 5) Manual pull apart openings for expandable batons
Factor 6) Spring release openings for expandable batons
Factor 7) Clothing
Factor 8) Length of arms for drawing and/or opening impact weapons
Factor 9) Space available to open and/or draw these weapons
Factor 10) ...and so on!

So each drill will have to contend with these differing factors. Pick a mission, a weapon, clothing you will wear, and a carry site, and experience quick draws with these following drills.

Impact Weapon QD Drill 1) Speed, Space and Stress Awareness Drills

Two training partners stand before each other, both armed with impact weapons. They go palm-to-palm. Draw and strike. They see who can draw and strike first, but this study goes deeper. Who-hits-who first is only a part. How many times they hit each other and where is more likely the end evaluation. Train with safety gear, and go after it hard core.

Round 1) Both have impact weapons
Round 2) Only one has a weapon. Unarmed fights back
Round 3) Both have weapons again, this time wiser

Impact Weapon QD Drill 2) Ground Quick Draws

The trainer is standing. The trainee is grounded. The trainer circles the downed trainee making attempts to jump on him or even kick him. The trainee spins to keep in a position to observe and kick his attacker. At some point, the attacker goes for his weapon. Drawing some impact weapons horizontally is different than standing and needs to be experienced. You need space to open expandable batons with momentum and to pull a fixed stick clear of your carrying system.

I ask that this drill begin with the trainee being punched or pushed down so that the trainee can experience this and learn to recover from it. The trainer should spend a few seconds circling the trainee so that the downed person can learn to maneuver on the ground.

Impact Weapon QD Drill 3) The Ground Roll Impact Weapon Quick Draw Drill

Here we are again, using the ground roll format. Start in any ground position and assign the trainee to draw and strike when possible. An unforgettable practice. Experiment with the many different kinds of weapons. See what can be done with what, under what circumstances. You will learn that expandable batons need some space and free arm movement to open.

Draw the stick and drive an end into the rib cage with a DMS grip or a choked up SMS One-Hand Grip. Grind it. The sharper the ends, the better. Use your body to push the enemy off.

Draw the stick and trench into the scalp, ears or face. The sharper your stick ends, the better.

You can use your unopened expandable baton as a palm stick-like striking device if you cannot get the space, time and momentum to open the weapon. There is a complete set of study using the closed baton along with the closed tactical folder. It will be presented in subsequent *CQCG Training Mission* books.

Impact Weapon QD Drill 4) Block, Pass and Pin Quick Draw Drill
A practitioner can develop extreme close quarter, one-handed quick draws by many ways but the following is a two-person drill inspired by martial art systems. This block, pass and pin synergy drill takes the exact same six steps, or beats, between two partners that was previously introduced in the unarmed combatives portion of this book. Partners first master the six steps/beats and then executes half-beat inserts – in this case impact weapon quick draws where possible. After reviewing the six steps, or beats, you quick draw on beat 3 1/2.

On beat 3 1/2 push hard, draw and open your impact weapon.

You must practice this format further as:

Variation 1) Draw on other half-beats.

Variation 2) Draw from cross draw carries.

Variation 3) The opponent really charges back at you to interfere with your draw.

Variation 4) Experiment by using differing impact weapons. See what can work.

Variation 5) Perform the drill on your back.

Variation 6) Invent new variables.

This is a great drill to experiment and develop impact weapon quick draws. It simulates very close, forearm-to-forearm conflict and gives a practitioner familiarity with this common combat crash and clash. Each variation is like a testing ground to give you experience in what you like and don't like and what you think you can get away with. Remember, you have to decide if you should, or even can, quick draw the weapon. Often you must simply fight with your empty hands. If you do pull the weapon and the opponent is unarmed, you may try a command presence order or bluff.

Impact Weapon QD Drill 5) Walking and Running Quick Draws
The trainee starts from a distance. He approaches the trainer at a walking pace or a running pace. The trainer draws, and the trainee must respond with a draw and fire while in motion.

As previously described in the pistol quick draw section, this drill covers the ability to draw a fixed or expandable baton while moving. Walk or run toward a trainer. The trainer will give you a cue to draw your weapon. The best cue is drawing his weapon. While moving, draw and prepare to fight. For advanced training, run straight to the trainer and engage in a combat scenario or freestyle sparring.

Impact Weapon Quick Draw Option Awareness Combat Scenarios

Practice these option awareness scenarios to develop the stress quick draw.

Impact Weapon QD CS 1a) Interview Stance – A Sample Study

Here you need to draw your stick from a belt carry. The following steps are a quick draw taught to many law enforcement officers in the United States.

The enemy moves. In this practice scenario, you draw and strike from the carry position with as hard a strike as possible.

Switch hands through a DMS transition.

Present the weapon to strike with a command presence, or strike a vital, effective target.

CS 1a) Practice a block, draw and stick strike.
CS 1b) Practice a hand strike, draw and stick strike.
CS 1c) Practice a push, draw and stick strike.

Impact Weapon QD CS 2) Stick vs. the Unarmed Criminal – A Sample Study

Many citizens and police officers find themselves in a dangerous confrontation standing before an agitated or crazed person, or a criminal. Your instinct, gut reaction and common sense will tell you to pull your weapon. You need an edge. You are not the aggressor. You have the tools on you to fight back successfully. You draw your impact weapon. You are armed and ready, and he is not armed. You bluff. Your command presence may work. But if it doesn't and you must take action, on paper, it is not a fair fight and could raise several legal issues should you seriously bash him. Certainly if you are an enforcement officer. Here is a sample scenario of dealing with this encounter.

The enemy stands before you and you quick draw. He takes the standard boxing pose.

You strike that lead fist with all your force. This will severely hurt most people, and...

...cause them to clutch the wounded hand with their other hand, an instinctive move.

This brings the other hand right up into the target zone. Bash it also.

A quick snap to the face if need be.
Finish as you see fit.

Impact Weapon QD CS 3) Stick versus the Choker – A Sample Study
Hundreds of counters to this choke? Yes, but we look here at our subject matter and illustrate an impact weapon response.

He chokes. You draw. You expand. Hit his nose on the way down to break the choke with an arm smash.
With this pulling in, suddenly smash forward into the teeth or rest of the face. Finish as needed.

CQC Group Level 1 Written Test

1) Name any three main finger attacks.
 1)_____
 2)_____
 3)_____

(Hooking)
(Thrusting)
(Pinching)
(Fish hook pulls)
(Twists)

2) Name the UC skill developing training tools.
 1)_____
 2)_____
 3)_____
 4)_____ to best develop the complete fighter.

(C&M in the air)
(C&M on objects)
(Synergy drills)
(Combat scenarios)

3) Name the three body positions required in training.
 1)_____
 2)_____
 3)_____

(Standing)
(Kneeling)
(On the ground)

4) Real world ground fighting requires more
_____ & _____ than wrestling.

(Kicking & Striking)

5) The fingers can be cranked in _____ ways.

(5)

6) Combat scenarios should include practice in:
 1)_____
 2)_____
 3)_____
 4)_____ problems.

(Hand)
(Stick)
(Knife)
(Gun)

7) All your combat action should be based upon:
 1)_____
 2)_____
 3)_____ standards.

(Moral)
(Ethical)
(Legal)

8) Versus a gun threat and a gun grab do you...
 (Circle one)
  1) grab as much of the gun as possible?
  2) grab as much of the hand as possible?

(yes)
(no)

9) Inside many takedowns and throws are:
_____

(Body joint crankings)

10) Name any three body parts a frontal snapping
 kick can strike with:
  1)_____
  2)_____
  3)_____

(Shoe toe)
(Instep)
(Shin)

CQC Group Level 1 Written Test

1) Name any three main finger attacks.
      1)_____
      2)_____
      3)_____

(Hooking)
(Thrusting)
(Pinching)
(Fish hook pulls)
(Twists)

2) Name the UC skill developing training tools.
      1)_____
      2)_____
      3)_____
      4)_____ to best develop the complete fighter.

(C&M in the air)
(C&M on objects)
(Synergy drills)
(Combat scenarios)

3) Name the three body positions required in training.
      1)_____
      2)_____
      3)_____

(Standing)
(Kneeling)
(On the ground)

4) Real world ground fighting requires more
_____&_____ than wrestling.

(Kicking & Striking)

5) The fingers can be cranked in _____ ways.

(5)

6) Combat scenarios should include practice in:
      1)_____
      2)_____
      3)_____
      4)_____ problems.

(Hand)
(Stick)
(Knife)
(Gun)

7) All your combat action should be based upon:
      1)_____
      2)_____
      3)_____ standards.

(Moral)
(Ethical)
(Legal)

8) Versus a gun threat and a gun grab do you...
  (Circle one)
      1) grab as much of the gun as possible?
      2) grab as much of the hand as possible?

(yes)
(no)

9) Inside many takedowns and throws are:

_____

(Body joint crankings)

10) Name any three body parts a frontal snapping
    kick can strike with:
      1)_____
      2)_____
      3)_____

(Shoe toe)
(Instep)
(Shin)

11) The mechanical three layers of "Working the Gun" are:

    1)_____   (Knowledge of weapon function)

    2)_____   (Knowledge of ammo)

    3)_____   (Marksmanship)

12) The four basic gun safety rules are:

    1)_____   (All guns are loaded.)

    2)_____   (Never point one unless you have a need to destroy and are committed to destroy.)

    3)_____   (Finger off the trigger until shooting.)

    4)_____   (Be sure of your target and beyond.)

13) Real quick draws are performed under_____.   (Combat stress)

14) The shooter who gets to _____ first is the one who statistically survives the most often.   (Cover)

15) _____ does not stop bullets.   (Concealment)

16) Good_____ stops bullets.   (Cover)

17) Some retention holsters may be difficult to draw from in _____ _____ positions.   (Ground fighting)

18) Name two uses of a sling on a long gun.

    1)_____   (Stand-down shoulder carry)

    2)_____   (Shooting support)

                              (tourniquet)

19) Two reasons to transition weapons from long gun to pistol, or vice-versa.   (out of ammo)

                              (need more or less firepower)

    1)_____   (malfunction of a weapon)

    2)_____   (small quarters search)

20) Name the two reasons to quick draw.   (prevent violence before...)

    1)_____   (stop violence while...)

    2)_____

21) Name the three main weapon carry sites.

    1)_____   (primary/quick draw)

    2)_____   (secondary/back-up)

    3)_____   (tertiary/lunge and reach)

22) Name the two types of enemies.

    1)_____   (criminals)

    2)_____   (enemy soldiers)

23) Name any 2 impact weapon pre-fight stances.

    1)_____   (Concealed saber grip)

    2)_____   (Concealed reverse grip)

                                             (Port Arms)

                                             (Parade Rest)

24) Expandable batons are illegal in _____ states and countries.   (many)

25) List the CQCG four ways of learning.

    1)_____   (C&M in the air)

    2)_____   (C&M on objects)

    3)_____   (Partner training)

    4)_____   (Psychology of violence study)

26) List the 5 main hand grips on impact weapons.

    1)_____   (One hand, one end)

    2)_____   (One hand, center)

    3)_____   (Two hands, one end "sword")

    4)_____   (Two hands, one on each end)

    5)_____   (Hybrid for odd shaped)

True/False

27)____All finger-to-eye attacks cause permanent blindness.   (F)

28)____We must completely rid our mind of emotions such as empathy.   (F)

29)____No one can predict with certainty what a body will do when shot, stabbed or struck.   (T)

30)____Gunfighters must learn to shoot while being shot at to best develop combat skills.   (T)

31)____Criminals average a 90 percent hit ratio in criminal/officer shootings.   (T)

32)____Some 40 percent of police shootings involve two or more opponents.   (T)

33)____Always access your gun sights when shooting, all the time.   (F)

34)____Always shoot pistols with a two-handed grip.   (F)

Instructor Notes, Advise and Observations:

23) Name any 2 impact weapon pre-fight stances.

    1)_____

    2)_____

(Concealed saber grip)
(Concealed reverse grip)
(Port Arms)
(Parade Rest)

24) Expandable batons are illegal in _____ states and countries.

(many)

25) List the CQCG four ways of learning.

    1)_____

    2)_____

    3)_____

    4)_____

(C&M in the air)
(C&M on objects)
(Partner training)
(Psychology of violence study)

26) List the 5 main hand grips on impact weapons.

    1)_____

    2)_____

    3)_____

    4)_____

    5)_____

(One hand, one end)
(One hand, center)
(Two hands, one end "sword")
(Two hands, one on each end)
(Hybrid for odd shaped)

True/False

27)____All finger-to-eye attacks cause permanent blindness. (F)

28)____We must completely rid our mind of emotions such as empathy. (F)

29)____No one can predict with certainty what a body will do when shot, stabbed or struck. (T)

30)____Gunfighters must learn to shoot while being shot at to best develop combat skills. (T)

31)____Criminals average a 90 percent hit ratio in criminal/officer shootings. (T)

32)____Some 40 percent of police shootings involve two or more opponents. (T)

33)____Always access your gun sights when shooting, all the time. (F)

34)____Always shoot pistols with a two-handed grip. (F)

Instructor Notes, Advise and Observations:

DEDICATION

This book is dedicated to Staff Sergeant Thomas Gaston, (U.S. Army, RET.), combat veteran of both the Korean and Vietnam Wars, whom I served under in South Korea in the mid 1970's. His experience, sense of humor and unique NCO leadership skills were a major influence in my personal and professional life.

...and to...

"The girl with the golden hair, she is my inspiration. She helps to set the mood."
Leslie West, Mountain

Special Thanks

Thanks to Photographer Rick Owens, Editors Jane Eden and Thomas Pentzer, Stuntmen Ronny Young, Tom Pierce, Darren Bogner, Keith Terry, Mike Gillette and Tom Barnhart.

CPSIA information can be obtained
at www.ICGtesting.com
Printed in the USA
LVOW09s0356100118
562494LV00005B/22/P